Philip Hunton

A Treatise of Monarchy

Containing two parts. I. Concerning monarchy in general. II. Concerning this particular monarchy, also a vindication of the said treatise

Philip Hunton

A Treatise of Monarchy
Containing two parts. I. Concerning monarchy in general. II. Concerning this particular monarchy, also a vindication of the said treatise

ISBN/EAN: 9783337244170

Printed in Europe, USA, Canada, Australia, Japan

Cover: Foto ©ninafisch / pixelio.de

More available books at **www.hansebooks.com**

A TREATISE OF MONARCHY:

Containing Two PARTS.

I. Concerning *Monarchy in General.*
II. Concerning *This Particular Monarchy.*

ALSO A VINDICATION Of the said TREATISE.

Done by an earnest Desirer of his Countries Peace.

LONDON,
Printed for *E. Smith*, and are to be Sold by *Randal Taylor*, near *Stationers-Hall*, 1689.

Reader,

THis *Treatise of Monarchy* was first Published in the Year 1643. and the Author in 1644, put forth a Vindication in Answer to Dr. *Ferns* Reply. The whole of the former is here Re-printed; and all of the latter, except what is Personal or Repetition. And this Information is given, that thou maist avoid imperfect Editions, such as that which was very lately Printed for *Richard Baldwin*.

Part. 1. Of Monarchy in General.

Chap. 1. Of Political Government.

Sect. 1. *Its Original: How far forth it is from God?* page 1
   2. *Its end: whether the end of government be the peoples good?* 4
   3. *Its division into several sorts.* ibid.
Chapter 2. *Of the division of Monarchy into absolute and limited.* 5
Sect. 1. *Whether absolute Monarchy be a lawful Government?* ibid.
   2. *Of three degrees of absoluteness in Monarchy.* 6
   3. *Whether Resistance be lawful in absolute Monarchy?* ibid.
   4. *What it is which constituteth a Monarchy limited?* 9
   5. *How far subjection is due in a limited Monarchy? Objections answered.* 11
   6. *How far resistance is lawful in a limited Monarchy?* 12
   7. *Who shall be Judge of the excesses of a limited Monarch?* 13
Chapter 3. *Of the division of Monarchy into Elective and Successive.* 15
Sect. 1. *Elective and successive Monarchies, what they are?* ibid.
   2. *Whether all Monarchy be originally from the peoples consent?* ibid.
   3. *Of Monarchy by divine Institution* 16.
   4. *Of Monarchy by Prescription.* ibid.
   5. *Of Monarchy by Conquest.* ibid.
     Whether Conquest can give a just Title? 17
   6. *Whether a successive Monarch may not be also limited?* 18
Chapter 4. *Of the division of Monarchy into simple and mixed.* 19
Sect. 1. *Simple and mixed Monarchy what they are?* 20
   2. *What it is which constituteth a Monarchy mixed.* 20
     Objections answered. 21
   3. *How farre the Princes power extends in a mixed Monarchy?* 23

Part. 2. Of this Particular Monarchy.

Chap. 1. *Whether the power wherewith our Kings be invested be an absolute or limited and moderated Power?* 25
Sect. 1. *The Question Stated.* ibid.
   2. *Proved radically limited.* ibid
   3, 4. *Contrary Arguments Answered.* 28, 29
Chap. 2. *Wherein and how this Monarchy is limited and defined?* 31
Chap. 3. *Whether it be of a simple or mixed constitution?* 32
Sect. 1. *It is proved to be fundamental mixed.* 33
   2. *The Arguments for the contrary are answered.* 34
   3. *Whether the Authority of the two Houses be subordinate and derived from the Kings?* 35

Sect. 4.

   4. *The Question resolved and cleared.* 35
Chap. 4. *How far forth this Monarchy is* **mixed**, *and what part of the power is referred to a mixed subject?* 37
Chap. 5. *How farr forth the two estates may oppose the Will and proceedings of the Monarch?* 39
Sect. 1, 2. *The Question duly stated.* 39
   3. *Whether Resistance of Instruments of illegal Commands be lawful?* 45
    Proved lawful. ibid.
   4. *Contrary Arguments dissolved.* 49
    Further objections answered. ibid.
Chap. 6. *In what cases the other Estates may assume the Arms of the Kingdom for resistance of Instruments of arbitrary Commands?*
Sect. 1. *Answered Negatively.* 52
   2. *Affirmatively.* 55
Chap. 7. *Where the legal power of final Judging of these cases doth reside, the Three Estates differing about them?* 56
Sect. 1. *The Question is stated and determined.* ibid.
   2. *Arguments contrary are answered.* 57
   3. *What to be done in such dissention.* 59
Chap. 8. Sect. 1. *The former Truths brought home to the present contention.* 60
   2. *A moderate debate concerning the present contention.* 61
   3. *The speediest means of Reconcilement proposed.* 63

The Contents of the Vindication.

Chap. 1. **W***Herein the vanity and falshood of the supposals, whereon some do build their discourses is made appear.*
Chap. 2. *Concerning the Constitution of this Monarchy, its Original, the Limitation and mixture of it Vindicated.*
Chap. 3. *Of Resistance in Relation to several kinds of Monarchy.*
Chap. 4. *Of places of Scripture out of the Old Testament.*
Chap. 5. *Concerning Resistance forbidden,* Rom. 13. *and the Reasons for and against Resistance Considered.*

A TREATISE OF MONARCHY.

PART I.

CHAP. I.
Of Political Government, and its Distinction into several Kinds.

Sect. 1. Government and Subjection are Relatives, so that what is said of the One, may in proportion be said of the other: Which being so, it will be needless to treat of both: Because it will be easie to apply what is spoken of one to the other. Government is *Potestatis Exercitium*, the exercise of a Moral Power. One of these is the Root and Measure of the other; which if it exceed, is exorbitant, is not Government, but a Transgression of it. This Power and Government is differenced with respect to the Governed, to wit, a Family, which is called *Oeconomical*: Or a publick Society, which is called *Political*, or Magistracy. Concerning this Magistracy we will treat, 1. In general. 2. Of the principal kind of it.

In general concerning Magistracy. There are two things about which I find difficulty and difference, *viz.* The Original and the End.

First for the Original: There seem to be two extremes in Opinion; while some amplifie the Divinity thereof; others speak so slightly of it, as if there were little else but Humane Institution in it. I will briefly lay down my apprehensions

Authority, how far from God, how far from men.

prehenſions of the evident truth in this point; and it may be, things being clearly and diſtinctly ſet down, there will be no real ground for contrariety in this matter. Three things herein muſt neceſſarily be diſtinguiſhed, *viz.* 1. The Conſtitution of Power of Magiſtracy in general. 2. The Limitation of it to this or that kind. 3. The Determination of it to this or that Individual Perſon or Line.

For the firſt of theſe; 1. It is Gods expreſs Ordinance that in the ſocieties of Mankind, there ſhould be a Magiſtracy of Government. At firſt when there were but two, God ordained it, *Gen.* 3. 16. St. *Paul* affirms as much of the Powers that be, none excepted, *Rom.* 13. 1. 2. This Power where ever placed ought to be reſpected as a participation of divine Soveraignty, *Pſal.* 82. 1. 6. and every ſoul ought to be ſubject to it for the *Lords ſake*, 1 *Pet.* 2. 13. that is, for Conſcience ſake of Gods Ordinance, *Rom.* 13. 5. and under penalty of Damnation, *v.* 2. Theſe are Truths againſt which there is no colour of oppoſition. Indeed this Power may be claimed by them who have it not; and where there is a limitation of this Power, ſubjection may be claimed in caſes which are without thoſe limits: But to this Ordinance of Power where it is, and when it requires ſubjection it muſt be given; as before.

For the ſecond. 1. In ſome particular communities the Limitation of it to this or that kind, is an immediate Ordinance of God; ſo Kingly Power was appointed to the *Jews*, on their deſire, 1 *Sam.* 8. 9. whether they had not a kind of Monarchical Government before, I will not ſtand on it; but it is evident that then, on their earneſt deſire, God himſelf condeſcended to an eſtabliſhment of Regality in that ſtate. 2. But for a general binding Ordinance, God hath given no word, either to command or commend one kind above another (*a*): Men may according to their Relations to the form they live under, to their affections and judgments in divers reſpects, prefer this or that form above the reſt; but we have no divine limitation; and it were an abſurdity to think ſo; for then we ſhould uncharitably condemn all the Communities which have not that form for violation of Gods Ordinance, and pronounce thoſe other Powers unlawful. 3. This then muſt have another and lower Fountain to flow from, which can be no other then Humane. The higher Power is Gods Ordinance: That it reſideth in One, or more; in ſuch or ſuch a way is from humane deſignment: for when God leaves a matter indifferent, the reſtriction of this indifferency is left to ſecondary cauſes. And I conceive this is St. *Peters* meaning, when he calls Magiſtracy ἀνθρωπίνη κτίσις, Humane Creature; St. *Paul* calls it *Gods Ordinance*, becauſe the

(*a*) *The Scripture was not given to preſcribe frames of Policy, which are various, according to the diſpoſition of people: General Rules there are for Government, which being obſerved, particulars which fall under no ſetled Rule, are left to Reaſon and the poſitive Laws of Nations to determine.*

the Power is *Gods* : St. *Peter* calls it Humane Ordinance, becaufe the fpecification of it to this or that form, is from the focieties of Mankind. confefs it may be called a humane Creature, in regard of its fubject, which is a Man, or Men : or its End, which is to rule over Men for the good of Men, but the other feems more natural ; and it induces no difparagement to Authority, being fo underftood. But how ever you take that place, yet the thing affirmed ftands good, that God by no word binds any people to this or that form, till they by their own Act bind themfelves.

For the third ; the fame is to be faid of it as of the fecond : Some particular Men we find whom God was pleafed by his own immediate choife to inveft with this his Ordinance of Authority ; *Mofes, Saul, David* ; yea God by his immediate Ordinance determined the Government of that people to *Davids* pofterity, and made it fucceffive ; fo that that people, after his appointment and word was made known to them, and the room void by *Sauls* death, was as immediately bound by Divine Law to have *David*, and his Sons after him to be Magiftrates, as to Magiftracy it felf. But God hath not done fo for every people : *a fcriptum eft* cannot be alledged for the endowing this or that perfon or ftock with Soveraignty over a community : They alone had the priviledge of an extraordinary Word : All others have the ordinary and mediate hand of God to enthrone them : They attain this determination of Authority to their Perfons by the tacite and vertual, or elfe exprefs a formal confent of that Society of Men they govern, either in their own perfons, or the root of their fucceffion, as I doubt not, in the fequel it will be made appear. But let no man think that it is any leffening or weakning of Gods Ordinance in them, to teach that it is annexed to their perfons by a humane Mean : For though it be not fo full a Title to come to it by the fimple Providence of God, as by the exprefs Precept of God ; yet when by the difpofing hand of Gods Providence a Right is conveyed to a perfon or family, by the means of a publick Fundamental Oath, Contract and Agreement of a State, it is equivalent then to a Divine Word ; and within the bounds of that publick Agreement ; the conveyed Power is as *Obligatory*, as if an immediate word had defigned it. Thus it appears that they which fay there is *divinum quiddam* in Sovereigns, and that they have their power from God, fpeak in fome fence Truth ; as alfo they which fay that originally Power is in the People (*b*), may in a found fence be underftood. And in thefe things we have Dr. *Ferns* confent in his late Difcourfe upon this fubject, Sect. 3.

(*b*) When we fay Power is in the People, we do not thereby deny it to be from God, as if Subordinates did exclude one another. God hath Ordained that Power fhould be : People by vertue of that Ordinance give them exiftence in this or that kind and fubject : And here note, if you will not have Limitation of Power to be at all from the People, how come you to admit the limitation of the Power to feveral kinds as from them. Is not limitation of it into kinds, limitation of the Power it felf ? but of this in a more proper place.

Of Political Government. Part 1.

Wnether the end of Government be the peoples good?

Sect. 2. For the end of Magistracy; to set out that is no hard matter, if we consider what was looked at when God ordained it. That was the good of the society of men over which it is set: So Saint *Paul, Rom.* 13. 4. οτι εις το ἀγαθόν. God aimed at it in the Institution of Government; and so do all men in the choice of it, where they may be choosers; such a Government, and such persons to sway it as may most conduce to publick Weal. Also it is the measure of all the Acts of the Governour; and he is good or bad according as he uses his Power to the good of the State wherewith he is intrusted. That is the end, but not the sole end: The preservation of the Power and Honour of the Governour is an end too; but I think not co-ordinate but subordinate to the other: because doubtless in the Constitution of Government, that is first thought on, and this in congruity to that: Also the reason why the Power and Honour of the Magistrate must be preserved, is for the publick Societies sake, because its welfare depends thereon: And if it fall out that one of them must suffer, every good Magistrate will descend something from his greatness, be it for the good of the Community: On the other side, though every Subject ought for the honour and good of the Magistrate to give up his private; yet none ought to advance the greatness of his Sovereign with the publick detriment. Whence in my apprehension the end of Magistracy is the good of the whole Body, Head, and Members conjunctly; but if we speak *divisim*, then the good of the Society is the ultime end; and next to that, as conducent to that, the Governours Greatness and Prerogative. And herein also accordeth Dr. *Fern* with us, *Sect.* 3. Where he sayes, That the people are the end of the governing Power. There is another question of mainer concernment, here in our general Discourse of Authority fitly to be handled; *viz.* How far subjection is due to it? But because it hath a great dependance on the kinds and states of Power, and cannot be so well conceived without the pretognition thereof: I will refer it to after opportunities.

Division of Magistracy.

Sect. 3. For the division of this Power of Magistracy. It cannot be well divided into several species, for it is one simple thing, an indivisible beam of Divine Perfection; yet for our more distinct conceiving thereof, Men have framed several distinctions of it. So with respect of its measure, it is absolute or limited: In respect of its manner, It is as St. *Peter* divides it, Supream or Subordinate. In respect of its Mean of acquiring, it is Elective or Successive; for I conceive that of Conquest and prescription of usage are reducible to one of these, as will appear afterwards. In respect of its degrees, it is *Nomothetical* or *Architectonical*, and *Gubernative* or *Executive*. And in respect of the subject of its residence there is an ancient and usual distinction of it into *Monarchical, Aristocratical* and *Democratical*.

These either simple, or mixt of two, or all three together, of which the *Predominant* gives the denomination. These are not *accurate specificative*, divisions of Power, for it admits none such, but partitions of it according to divers respects. The course of my intention directs me to speak only of *Monarchical Power*, which is the chief, and most usual form of Government in the World: The other two being apt to resolve into this, but this not so apt to dissolve into them.

CHAP. II.

Of the Division of Monarchy into absolute and limited.

Sect. 1. NOW we must know that most of those distinctions which were applyed to Power in general are applyable to Monarchy; because the respects on which they arise are to be found in it. But I will insist on the three main divisions; for the handling of them will bring us to a clear understanding of what is needful to be known about *Monarchical Power*.

First, Of the distinction of *Monarchy* into Absolute and Limited. Absolute *Monarchy* is when the Soveraignty is so fully in one, that it hath no Limits or Bounds under God, but his own Will. It is when a people are absolutely resigned up, or resign up themselves to be governed by the will of one Man. Such were the ancient *Eastern Monarchies*, and that of the *Persian* and *Turk* at this day, as far as we know. This is a Lawful Government, and therefore where men put themselves into this utmost degree of subjection by *Oath* and *Contract*, or are born and brought unto it by Gods Providence, it binds them and they must abide it, because an *Oath* to a Lawful thing is *Obligatory*. This in Scripture is very evident, as *Ezek.* 17. 16, 18, 19. Where Judgment is denounced against the King of *Judah*, for breaking the Oath made to the King of *Babylon*; and it is called Gods Oath; yet doubtless this was an Oath of absolute subjection. And *Rom.* 1. 3. the Power which then was, was absolute; yet the Apostle not excluding it, calls it *Gods Ordinance*, and commands subjection to it; so Christ commands Tribute to be paid, and payes it himself; yet it was an Arbitrary Tax, the production of an Absolute Power. Also the Soveraignty of Masters over Servants was absolute, and the same in Oeconomy as absolute Monarchy is in Policy, yet the Apostle enjoyns not Masters called to Christianity to renounce that title as too great and rigid to be kept;

Whether Absolute Monarchy be a lawful Government.

but

but exhorts them to moderation in the exercise of it; and servants to remain contented in the condition of their servitude. More might be said to Legitimate this kind of Government, but it needs not in so plain a Case.

Three degrees of Absoluteness. Sect. 3. This absolute Monarchy hath three degrees, yet all within the state of absoluteness. The first, when the Monarch, whose Will is the peoples Law, doth set himself no stated Rule or Law to rule by, but by immediate Edicts and Commands of his own Will governs them, as in his own and Councels judgment he thinks fit. Secondly, When he sets down a Rule and Law by which he will ordinarily govern, reserving to himself liberty to vary from it, wherein, and as oft as in his discretion he judges fit; and in this the Sovereign is as free as the former, only the people are at a more certainty what he expects from them in ordinary. Thirdly, When he not only sets down an express Rule and Law to govern by, but also promiseth and engages himself in many cases not to alter that Rule; but this engagement is an after condescent and Act of Grace, not dissolving the absolute Oath of subjection which went before it, nor is intended to be the Rule of his Power, but of the Exercise of it. This Ruler is not so absolute as the former in the use of his Power, for he hath put a Bond on that, which he cannot break without breach of promise, that is, without sin; but he is as absolute in his Power, if he will sinfully put it forth into act, it hath no politick bounds, for the people still owe him absolute subjection, that not being dissolved or lessened by an Act of Grace coming afterwards.

Whether resistance be lawful in absolute Monarchy. Sect. 3. Now in Governments of this nature, how far Obedience is due, and whether any Resistance be Lawful, is a question which here must be decided. For the due effecting whereof, we must premise some needful distinctions to avoid confusion. Obedience is twofold; First, positive and active, when in Conscience of an Authority we do the thing commanded: Secondly, Negative and passive, when though we answer not Authority by doing, yet we do it by contented undergoing the penalty imposed. Proportionably Resistance is twofold: First, Positive, by an opposing of Force: Secondly, Negative, when only so much is done as may defend our selves from Force, without return of Force against the Assailant. Now this negative Resistance is also twofold: First, In inferiour and sufferable cases: Secondly, Or in the supream case and last necessity of Life and Death; and then too it is first, either of particular person or persons: Secondly, Or of the whole community. And if of particular persons, then either under plea and pretence of equity assaulted; or else without any plea at all, meerly for will and pleasure sake; for to that degree of rage and cruelty sometimes the heart of man is given over. All these are very distinguishable cases, and will be of use either in this or the insuing disputes.

Assert. 1. To the question I say. First, Positive obedience is absolutely due to the will and pleasure of an absolute Monarch, in all lawful and indifferent things: because in such a State the will of the Prince is the supreme Law, so that it binds to obedience in every thing not prohibited by a superiour, that is Divine Law: for it is in such case the higher power, and is Gods Ordinance.

Assert. 2. Secondly, When the will of an absolute Monarch commands a thing forbidden to be done by Gods Law then it binds not to active obedience; then is the Apostles rule undoubtedly true, *It is better to obey God then Men:* For the Law of the inferiour gives place to the superiour. In things defined by God, it should be all one with us for the Magistrate to command us to transgress that, as to command us an impossibility; and impossibilities fall under no Law. But on this ground no man must quarrel with Authority, or reject its commands as unlawful, unless there be an open unlawfulness in the face of the act commanded. For if the unlawfulness be hidden in the ground or reason of the action, inferiours must not be curious to enquire into the grounds or reasons of the commands of superiours; for such licence of enquiry would often frustrate great undertakings, which much depend on speed and secrecy of execution. I speak all this of absolute Government, where the will and reason of the Monarch is made the higher power, and its expression the supreme Law of a state.

Assert. 3. Thirdly, suppose an absolute Monarch should so degenerate into Monstrous unnatural Tyranny, as apparently to seek the destruction of the whole community, subject to him in the lowest degree of vassallage, then such a community may negatively resist such subversion: yea, and if constrained to it by the last necessity, positively resist and defend themselves by force against any instruments whatsoever, imployed for the effecting thereof. 1. *David* did so in his particular case, when pursued by *Saul*: he made negative resistence by flight, and doubtless he intended positive resistence against any instrument, if the negative would not have served the turn: else why did he so strengthen himself by Forces? sure not to make positive resistance, and lay violent hands upon the Person of the Lords Anointed, as it appeared; yet for some reason he did it doubtless, which could be none other, but by that force of Arms to defend himself against the violence of any mis-imployed inferiour hands. If then he might do it for his particular safety, much rather may it be done for the publick. 2. Such an act is without the compass of any of the most absolute Potentate; and therefore to resist in it, can be to resist no power, nor the violation of any due of subjection. For, first, the most submiss subjection ever intended by any community, when they put themselves under anothers power, was the command of a reasonable

able will and power; but to will and command the destruction of the whole body over which a power is placed, were an act of will most unreasonable and self-destructive, and so not the act of such a will, to which subjection was intended by any reasonable Creatures. Secondly, the publick good and being is aimed at in the utmost bond of subjection; for in the constitution of such unlimited soveraignty, though every particular mans good and being is subjected to the will of One supreme, yet certainly the conservation of the whole publick was intended by it; which being invaded, the intent of the constitution is overthrown, and an act is done which can be supposed to be within the compass of no political power: So that did *Nero* as it was reported of him in his immanity thirst for the destruction of whole *Rome*; and if he were truly what the Senate pronounced him to be, *Humani generis hostis*, then it might justifie a negative resistance of his person; and a positive, of any Agent should be set on so inhumane a service. And the United Provinces are allowed in resisting *Philip* 2*d*. though he had been their absolute Monarch, if he resolved the extirpation of the whole people, and the planting the countrey with *Spaniards*, as it is reported he did. And that assertion of some, that *All* resistance is against the Apostles prohibition. Resistance by power of Arms is utterly unlawful, cannot be justified in such a latitude. But of this more will be spoken in the current of this discourse.

Assert. 4. Fourthly, suppose by such a power any particular person or persons life be invaded, without any plea of reason or cause for it, I suppose it hard to deny him liberty of negative resistance of power; yea, and positive, of any Agents in such assault of murther: for though the case be not so clear as the former yet it seems to me justified by the fact of *David*, and the rescuing of *Jonathan* from the causless cruel intent of his Fathers putting him to death. As also such an act of will carrying no colour of reason with it, cannot be esteemed the act of a rational will, and so no will intended to be the Law of soveraignty. Not that I think a Monarch of such absoluteness is bound to yeild a reason why he commands any man to be put to death, before his command be obeyed; but I conceive the person so commanded to death may be justified before God and men, for protecting himself by escape, or otherwise, unless some reason or cause be made known to him of such command.

Assert. 5. Fifthly, Persons subject to an unlimited dominion must without resistance subject their Estates, Liberties, Persons, to the will and pleasure of their Lord, so it carry any plea or shew of reason and equity. First, it seems to me evident, 1 *Pet.* 2. 18, 19, 20 if well doing be mistaken by the reason and judgment of the power for ill doing, and we be punished for it, yet the Magistrate going according to his misguided reason, it is the command of reasonable will, and so to be submitted to; because such a one suffers by Law, in a state where the Lords will is the Law. Secondly, In com-

commands of the power, where is the plea of reason and equity on the part of the commander, whether it be such indeed, some power must judge, but the constitution of absolute Monarchy resolves all judgement into the will of the Monarch, as the supreme Law: so that if his will judicially censure it just, it must be yeilded to as if it were just without repeal or redrefsment by any created power. And let none complain of this as a hard condition when they or their Ancestors have subjected themselves to such a power by oath, or political Contract: If it be Gods Ordinance to such, it must be subjected to and its exorbitances born, as he says in *Tacitus*, as men bear Famine, Pestilence, and other effects of Gods displeasure.

Assert. 6thly, in absolute Monarchy the person of the Monarch is above the reach of just force and positive resistance: for such a full resignation of mens selves to his will and power, by the irrevocable oath and bond of political Contract, doth make the person as sacred as the Unction of *Saul* or *David*. In such a State all lawful power is below him, so that he is uncapable of any penal hand, which must be from a superiour, or it is unjust (c). I have been the longer on this absolute Monarchy because though it doth not concern us, yet it will give light to the stating of doubts in Governments of a more restrained nature: for what is true here in the full extent of power, is there also as true within the compass of their power.

(c) *It is directly against the Word and all found reason, that a people lifting up a person above themselves, and by Sacred Covenant giving him a power above themselves, should afterwards on any pretence, assume a power of resisting that person and power, and violate their own Covenant and Oath of Subjection. But if that person be invested with a Limited Power: and he proceeds to acts of meer Arbitrariness without the limits of that power conferred on him; Then it is all the reason in the World, that the Limiting States should exercise an effectual restraining power by resisting instruments of such Arbitrary and subversive Acts, and we have not a sillable of Scripture contradicting it. Of which more hereafter.*

Sect. 4. In moderate or limited Monarchy it is an enquiry of some weight to know, *What it is which Constitutes it in the state of a limited Monarchy*.

What makes a Monarchy limited.

Assert. 1. First, A Monarchy may be stinted in the exercise of its power, and yet be an absolute Monarchy, as appeared before in our distinction of absolute Monarchy: If that bounds be a subsequent act, and proceeding from free will and grace in the Monarch: for it is not the exercise, but the nature and measure of power, wherewith he is radically invested, which denominates him a free, or conditionate Monarch.

Assert. 2. Secondly, I take it that a limited Monarch must have his bounds of power *ab externo*, not from the free determination of his own will. And now Kings have not divine words and binding Laws to constitute them in their Soveraignty, but derive it from ordinary Providence, the sole mean

C hereof

hereof is the confent and fundamental contract of a Nation of Men, which confent puts them in their power, which can be no more nor other then is conveyed to them by fuch contract of fubjection. This is the root of all foveraignty individuated and exiftent in this or that perfon or family; till this come and lift him up he is a private man, not differing in ftate from the reft of his brethren; but then he becomes another man, his perfon is facred by that foveraignty conveyed to it, which is Gods ordinance and image. The truth hereof will be more fully difcovered, when we come to fpeak of Elective and Succeffive Monarchy.

Affert. 3. Thirdly, He is then a limited Monarch, who hath a Law befide his own will for the meafure of his power. Firft, the fupreme power of the ftate muft be in him, fo that his power muft not be limited by any power above his; for then he were not a Monarch, but a fubordinate Magiftrate. Secondly, this fupreme power muft be reftrained by fome Law according to which this power was given, and by direction of which this power muft act; elfe he were not a limited Monarch, that is, a liege Soveraign or legal King. Now a Soveraignty comes thus to be legal, or defined to a rule of Law, either by original conftitution, or by after-condefcent. By original conftitution, when the fociety publick conferrs on one man a power by limited Contract, refigning themfelves to his government by fuch a Law, referving to themfelves fuch immunities: In this cafe, they which at firft had power over themfelves, had power to fet their own terms of fubjection; and he which hath no title of power over them but by their act, can *de jure* have no greater then what is put over to him by that act. By after-condefcent, *viz.* when a Lord, who by conqueft, or other right, hath an abfolute Arbitrary power; but not liking to hold by fuch a right, doth either formally or virtually defert it, and take a new legal right, as judging it more fafe for him to hold by, and defirable of the people to be governed by. This is equivalent to that by original conftitution; yea, is all one with it: for this is in that refpect a fecondary original conftitution. But if it be objected, that this being a voluntary condefcent is an act of grace, and fo doth not derogate from his former abfolutenefs, as was faid before of an abfolute Monarch, who confines himfelf to govern by one rule; I anfwer, This differs effentially from that: for there, a free Lord, of grace yields to rule by fuch a Law, referving the fulnefs of power, and ftill requiring of the people a bond and oath of utmoft indefinite fubjection; fo that it amounts not to a limitation of radical power: whereas here is a change of title, and a refolution to be fubjected to, in no other way, then according to fuch a frame of government; and accordingly no other bond or oath of Allegiance is required, or taken, then according to fuch a Law: this amounts to a limitation of radical power. And therefore they fpeak too generally, who affirm of all acts of grace proceeding from Princes to people, as if they did not limit abſoluteneſs: 'Tis true of acts of grace of that firſt kind; but yet you ſee an act of grace may be ſuch a one, as may amount to a reſignation of that abſoluteneſs, into a more mild and moderate power, unleſs we ſhould hold it out of the power of an abſolute Lord to be other, or that by free condeſcent, and act of grace, a man cannot as well part with, or exchange his right and title to a thing, as define himſelf in the uſe and exerciſe; which I think none will affirm.

Objection, *True, if ſuch a Monarch limits himſelf, and reſerve a power to vary, but if he fix a Law with promiſe not to vary, then in theſe caſes he is limited.*

Anſwer. Note, the fraud of this Replyer, he alters his terms and puts things as oppoſite which are not ſo. 1. He ſhould ſay if he limit himſelf, *and reſerve a power to vary,* then he is abſolute; but if he limit himſelf and *reſerve no power to vary,* (for then the oppoſition is direct) then he is limited; but inſtead of ſaying *(and reſerve no power to vary)* he ſays, but [*if he promiſe not to vary,*] I ſay that promiſe not to vary, if it be a ſimple promiſe of not varying, it doth not make him limited in his power any more than Morally and ſo every abſolute Monarch is limited. I affirm ſtill, it is a limitation of the *Power it ſelf,* not barely of the exerciſe, which conſtitutes a limited Monarch: for Monarchy is a ſtate of power, and therefore its ſpecificative deſtinction muſt be from ſomething which diſtinguiſheth powers, and not the exerciſe of powers.

2. Who ſees not that a *Promiſe,* whereby a Monarch may bind himſelf may either be with *a limitation* of the bond of ſubjection, or without: And that this makes a real difference, for in this the Government remains the ſame, becauſe the duty of ſubjection received no variation; but in that there is for ſo much a paſſing into a limited condition.

Objection, *Where there is ſuch a change of Title, it is done at once, and by expreſs and by notorious reſignation of former power, but it is not neceſſary that an abſolute Monarch ſhould come to a limited condition after that manner.*

Anſwer. If he will paſs into a limited Condition, it is neceſſary there be a limitation of his power, elſe he is not truly limited: but that all ſuch limitations be done *at once* and by *notorious Reſignation,* it is not neceſſary.

Sect. 5. In all Governments of this allay and legal Conſtitution, there are three Queſtions of ſpecial moment to be conſidered.

Firſt, How far ſubjection is due? As far as they are Gods Ordinance, as far as they are a Power, and they are a Power as far as the Contract Fundamental, from which under God their Authority is derived, doth extend. *How far ſubjection is due in a limited monarchy?*

As abſolute Lords muſt be obeyed as far as their Will enjoyns, becauſe their Will is the meaſure of their Power, and their Subjects Law; ſo theſe in the utmoſt extent of the Law of the Land, which is the meaſure of their

Power, and their Subjects duty of Obedience. I say so far, but I do not say no further; for I believe, though on our former grounds it clearly followes, that such Authority transcends its bounds if it command beyond the Law; and the subject legally is not bound to subjection in such case, yet in Conscience a subject is bound to yield to the Magistrate, even when he cannot *de jure*, challenge Obedience, to prevent scandal or any occasion of slighting the Power which may sometimes grow, even upon a just refusal: I say, for these causes a Subject ought not to use his Liberty, but *morem gerere*, if it be in a thing in which he can possibly without subversion, and in which his Act may not be made a leading case, and so bring on a prescription against publick Liberty.

Sest. 6. Secondly, How far it is Lawful to resist the exorbitant Illegal Commands of such a Monarch?

How far it is Lawful to resist.

Pos. 1. As before in lighter cases, in which it may be done, for the Reasons alledged, and for the sake of publick peace, we ought to submit, and make no resistance at all, but *de jure recedere*.

Pos. 2. In cases of higher nature passive resistance, *viz.* By appeal to Law, by Concealment, by Flight, is Lawful to be made, because such a Command is politically Powerless, it proceeds not from Gods Ordinance in him; and so we sin not against Gods Ordinance in such Non-submission, or Negative resistance.

Pos. 3. For Instruments or Agents in such commands; if the streight be such, and a Man be surprized, that no place is left for an appeal nor evasion by Negative resistance; I conceive, against such, Positive resistance may be made; because Authority failing of this Act in the Supream Power, the Agent or Instrument can have none derived to him; and so is but in the nature of a private person, and his Act, as an offer of private violence, and so comes under the same rules for opposition.

Pos. 4. For the Person of the Sovereign, I conceive it, as well above any Positive Resistance, as the Person of an absolute Monarch: Yea, though by the whole Community, (except there be an express reservation of Power in the body of the State, or any Deputed Persons or Court, to use (in case of intolerable exorbitance, positive Resistance,) which, if there be, then such a Governour is no Monarch, for that Fundamental Reservation destroys its being a Monarchy, in as much as the Supream Power is not in one.) For where ever there is a Sovereign politick Power constituted, the person or persons who are invested with it are Sacred, and out of the reach of positive Resistance or Violence; which, as I said, if just, must be from no inferiour or subordinate hand. But it will be objected, that sith every Monarch hath his Power from the consent of the whole Body, that consent of the whole Body hath a Power above the Power of the Monarch, and so the resistance which is done by it, is not by an inferiour power, and to this purpose is brought that Axiome, *Quicquid efficit tale est magis tale.* I answer, That Rule even in natural causes is lyable to abundance of restrictions: And in the particular in hand it holds not. Where the cause doth bereave himself of that perfection by which it works, in the very act of causing, and convey it to that effect; it doth not remain more such then the effect, but much less, and below it; as if I convey an Estate of Land to another, it doth not hold that after such conveyance I have a better Estate remaining in me then that other, but rather the contrary; because what was in one is passed to the other: The Servant who at the year of *Jubile* would not go out free, but have his Ear boared, and given his Master a full Lordship over him: Can we argue, that he had afterward more power over himself then his Master, because he gave his Master that power over him, by that act of Oeconomical Contract. Thus the Community, whose consent establishes a power over them, cannot be said universally to have an eminency of power above that which they constitute; sometimes they have, sometimes they have not; and to judge when they have, when not, respect must be had to the Original Contract and Fundamental Constitution of that State, if they have constituted a Monarchy, that is, invested one Man with the Sovereignty of power, and subjected all the rest to him: Then it were unreasonable to say, they yet have it in themselves; or have a power of recalling that Supremacy which by Oath and Contract they themselves transferred on another; unless we make this Oath and Contract less binding then private ones, dissoluble at pleasure, and so all Monarchs Tenants at will from their people. But if they in such Constitution reserve a power in the Body to oppose and displace the Magistrate for exorbitancies, and reserve to themselves a Tribunal to try him in, that Man is not a Monarch, but the Officer and Substitute of him or them to whom such power over him is reserved or conferred. The Issue is this; If he be a Monarch he hath the *Apex* or *Culmen Potestatis*, and all his Subjects *divisim* and *conjunctim*, are below him: They have devested themselves of all Superiority, and no power left for a positive opposition of the person of him whom they have invested.

Sect. 7. Thirdly, Who shall be the Judge of the Excesses of the Sovereign Lord in Monarchies of this composure? I answer, A frame of Government cannot be imagined of that perfection, but that some inconveniencies there will be possible, for which there can be provided no remedy: Many miseries to which a people under an absolute Monarchy are lyable, are prevented by this Legal allay and definement of power. But this is exposed to one defect from which that is free, that is an impossibility of constituting a Judge to determine this last Controversie, *viz.* The Sovereign

Who shall be the judge of the Excesses of the Monarch.

trans

tranfgreffing his Fundamental Limits. This Judge muft be either fome Forreigner, and then we lofe the freedom of the State, by fubjecting it to an external power in the greateft cafe; or elfe within the body: If fo, then 1. Either the Monarch himfelf, and then you deftroy the frame of the State, and make it abfolute; for to define a Power to a Law, and then to make him Judge of his Deviations from that Law, is to abfolve him from all Law. Or elfe, 2. The Community and their Deputies muft have this power; and then, as before, you put the *apex Poteftatis*, the *prime ἀρχεῖ* in the whole body, or a part of it, and deftroy the being of Monarchy: The Ruler not being Gods immediate Minifter, but of that Power, be it where it will, to which he is accountable for his actions. So that I conceive in a limited Legal Monarchy, there can be no ftated internal Judge of the Monarchs Actions, if there grow a Fundamental Variance betwixt him and the Community. But you will fay, It is all one way to Abfolutenefs, to affign him no Judge as to make him his own Judge. *Anfwer*, I fay not fimply in this cafe there is no Judge: But that there can be no Judge Legal and Conftituted within that frame of Government; but it is a tranfcendent cafe beyond the provifion of that Government, and muft have an axtraordinary Judge, and way of decifion.

In this great and difficult cafe, I will deliver my apprehenfions freely and clearly, fubmitting them to the cenfure of better Judgments. Suppofe the Controverfie to happen in a Government Fundamentally Legal, and the people no further fubjected then to Government by fuch a Law.

Pof. 1. If the act in which the exorbitance and tranfgreffion is fuppofed to be, be of leffer moment, and not ftriking at the very being of that Government, it ought to be born by publick patience, rather then to endanger the being of the State by a contention betwixt the Head and Body politick.

Pof. 2. If it be mortal, and fuch as fuffered, diffolves the frame and life of the Government and publick Liberty. Then the illegality and deftructive nature is to be fet open, and redrefment fought by Petition; which if failing, prevention by Refiftance ought to be. But firft that it is fuch muft be made apparent; and if it be apparent, and an Appeal made *ad confcientiam generis humani*, efpecially of thofe of that Community, then the Fundamental Laws of that Monarchy muft judge and pronounce the fentence in every Mans Confcience; and every Man, (as far as concerns him) muft follow the evidence of Truth in his own Soul, to oppofe, or not oppofe, according as he can in Confcience acquit or condemn the act of carriage of the Governour. For I conceive, in a Cafe which tranfcends the frame and provifion of the Government they are bound to, people are unbound, and in ftate as if they had no Government; and the fuperiour Law of Reafon and Confcience muft be Judge, wherein every one muft proceed

ceed with the utmost advice and impartiality: For if he err in judgment, he either resists Gods Ordinance, or puts his hand to the subversion of the State and Policy he lives in.

And this power of Judging argues not a Superiority in those who Judge, over him who is Judged; for it is not Authoritative and Civil, but Moral, residing in Reasonable Creatures, and Lawful for them to execute, because never devested and put off by any act in the constitution of a Legal Government, but rather the Reservation of it intended: For when they define the Superiour to a Law, and constitute no Power to Judge of his Excesses from that Law, it is evident they reserve to themselves, not a formal Authoritative Power, but a Moral Power, such as they had Originally before the constitution of the Government; which must needs remain, being not conveyed away in the constitution.

CHAP. III.

Of the division of Monarchy into Elective and Successive.

Sect. 1. THE Second division of Monarchy, which I intend to treat of, is that of Elective or Successive. Elective Monarchy is that, whereby the fundamental constitution of the State, the Supream Power is conveyed but to the person of him whom they take for their Prince; the people reserving to themselves power, by Men deputed by the same constitution, to elect a new person on the decease of the former. Successive is, where by the fundamental constitution of the State, the Sovereignty is conferred on one Prince; and in that one, as a root and beginning to his Heirs, after a form and line of Succession, constituted also by the Fundamentals of that Government. In the first, the peoples Oath and Contract of subjection extends but to one person: In the other, to the whole Race and Line of Successors, which continuing, the bond of subjection continues; or which failing the people return to their first liberty, of choosing a new person, or succession to be invested with Soveraignty. *Elective and successive monarchy what they are?*

Sect. 2. I do conceive that in the first original all Monarchy, yea, any individual frame of Government whatsoever, is Elective: that is, is Constituted, and draws its force and right from the consent and choice of that Community over which it swayeth. And that triple distinction of Monarchy into that which is gotten by Conquest, Prescription, or Choice, is, not of distinct parts unless by *All Monarchy whether originally from consent?*

Choice be meant full and formal Choice: my reason is because man being a voluntary agent, and subjection being a moral act it doth essentially depend on consent: so that a man may by force and extremity be brought under the power of another, as unreasonable creatures are, to be disposed of, and trampled on, whether they will or no: But a bond of subjection cannot be put on him, nor a right to claim Obedience and Service acquired, unless a man become bound by some act of his own Will. For, suppose another, from whom I am originally free, be stronger then I, and so bring me under his mercy, do I therefore sin if I do not what he commands me? or can that act of violence pass into a moral title, without a moral principle?

Monarchy by divine institution.   Sect. 3. But this will be more manifest, if by induction I shew how other titles resolve into this. I will begin with that of divine institution. *Saul* and *David* were by the Sacrament of anointing designed to the Kingdom, as it were by Gods own hand, which notwithstanding they were not actually Kings till the Peoples consent established them therein? that unction was a manifestation of the appointment of God, and when it was made known to the people, I think it had the power of precept to restrain the peoples choice to that person; which if they had not done, they had resisted Gods ordinance. Yet they were not thereby actually endowed with Kingly power, but remained as private men, till the peoples choice put them in actual possession of that power; which in *David* was not till after many years.

Monarchy by prescription.   Sect. 4. Then for that of Usuage or Prescription; if any such did ever constitute a Monarchy, it was by vertue of an Universal consent by that usuage and prescription proved and imployed: For in a popular state, where one Man in the Community, by reason of great estate, wisdom, or other perfection is in the eye of the all rest, all reverence him and his advice they follow: and the respect continues from the people to the house and family, for divers generations. In this case subjection at first is arbitrary in the people; and if in time it become necessary, it is because their Custom is their Law; and its long continuance is equivalent to a formal Election: so that this Tenure and Right, if it be good and more then at pleasure, as it was at first, the considerate must needs ascribe it to a consent and implicite choice of the people.

Monarchy by Conquest.   Sect. 5. But the main Question is concerning Monarchy atchieved by Conquest; where at first sight the Right seems gotten by the Sword, without the consent and Choice of the people, yea against it. Conquest is either 1. Total where a full Conquest is made, by a total subduing a people to the Will of the Victor: or 2. Partial, where an entrance is made by the Sword: But the people either because of the Right claimed by the Invader; or their unwillingness to suffer the Miseries of War, or their apparent inability to stand out in a way of Resistance, or some other consideration, submit to a composition and contract of subjection to the Invader. In this latter it is evident, the Sovereigns Power is from the Peoples consent; and the Government is such as the Contract and Fundamental Agreement makes it to be, if it be the first Agreement, and the pretender hath no former Title which remains in force, for then this latter is invalid, if it include not and amount to a relinquishing and disanulling of the Old. But the difficulty is concerning a full and meer Conquest; and of this I will speak my mind clearly. Such a War and Invasion of a People, which ends in a Conquest, 1. It is either upon the pretence or claim of a Title of Sovereignty over the People Invaded; and then if the pretender prevail, it is properly no Conquest, but the vindication of a Title by force of Armes. And the Government is not Original, but such as the Title is by which he claims it. 2. Or it is by One who hath no challenge of Right descending to him to justifie his Claim and Invasion of a People: Then if he subdue, he may properly be said to come to his Government by Conquest.

And there be who wholly condemn this title of Conquest as unlawful, and take it for nothing else but a National and publick robbery: So one of the Answerers to Doctor *Ferne* sayes in his p. 10. *Conquest may give such a right as Plunderers use to take in Houses they can master.* ——— *It is inhumane to talk of Right of Conquest in a Civil, in a Christian State.* But I cannot allow of so indefinite a Censure; rather I think the right of Conquest is such as the precedent War was: If that were Lawful, so is the Conquest: For a Prince may be invaded, or so far injured by a Neighbour people, or they may be set on such a pernicious enmity against him and his people, that the safety of himself and people may compel to such a War, which War if it in end in Conquest, who can judge such Title unlawful? Suppose then Conquest may be a lawful way of acquisition; yet an immediate cause of right of Sovereignty, that is, of a Civil Power of Government to which Obedience is due, it cannot be: I say, an immediate cause, for a remote impulsive cause it oft is, but not an immediate formal cause; for that must ever be the consent of the people, whereby they accept of, and resign up themselves to a Government, and then their persons are Morally bound, and not before. Thus far the force of Conquest may go; it may give a Man Title over, and Power to possess and dispose of the Countrey and Goods of the Conquered; yea the Bodies and Lives of the Conquered are at the Will and Pleasure of the Conquerour: But it still is at the Peoples choice to come into a moral condition of subjection or not. When they are thus at the Mercy of the Victor, if to save Life they consent to a Condition of Servitude or Subjection, then that Consent, Oath or Cove-

Whether Conquest gives just title?

nant, which they in that extremity make, being in *re licita*, binds them, and they owe Moral Duty. But if they would rather suffer the utmost violence of the Conquerour, and will consent to no termes of subjection, as *Numantia* in *Spain*, and many other people have resolved; they dye or remain a free People. Be they captived or possessed at pleasure, they owe no Duty, neither do they sin in not obeying; nor do they resist Gods Ordinance, if at any time of advantage they use Force to free themselves from such a violent possession; yea, perhaps, if before by Contract they were bound to another, they should sin, if to avoid Death or Bondage they should Swear or Covenant Fealty to a Conquerour; and it were more noble and laudable to dye in the service, and for the Faith to their Natural Sovereign.

I grant a people (not pre-obliged) fully overcome should much sin against Gods Providence by obstinacy, if on a meer Will, they consent not to reasonable terms of Subjection: But this I say, there is no Moral Obligation to Authority, before that Consent bind them: Conquest may be an *Antecedent Cause*; but the *immediate and formal Cause* is only the Consent of the People; for that must be *Moral* and not meerly *Violent*. The call of Providence challengeth a contented submission, if there be no reason hindering it; but if a precedent Oath, or some other sound Reason intervene, then it is no Call requiring submission; neither can the fullest Conquest make a people Debtors, but they remain free from any Moral Bond; for the Providence of God being of it self external, can indure no Moral State: But that Providence which on one discovery calls to a submission; on a like discovery may free them again, if nothing else come between, to render them Morally bound. A *Traveller* by the Providence of God shut up into the hands of a *Robber*, hath his life and protection promised him in his journey, if he will promise to pay him so much Money: I say, this Traveller should sin against his own Life, and the Providence of God, offering him those terms, if obstinately he refuse submission: Yet no man will say he owes the Robber so much Money because he hath him at his Mercy, until he by promise make himself a Debtor:

Thus I am perswaded it will appear an uncontroulable truth in Policy, that the consent of the people, either by themselves or their Ancestors is the only mean in ordinary providence by which Sovereignty is conferred on any Person or Family; neither can Gods Ordinance be conveyed, and people engaged in Conscience by any other means.

Whether a Monarchy by succession may not be limited

Sect. 6. It hath been affirmed by some, that mixture and limitation is inconsistent to successive Monarchy: as if where ever Sovereignty is entailed to a Succession, it must needs be Absolute. But I must profess I cannot see how it can stand with Truth: Rather I think, that both Elective and

Hereditary Monarchy are indifferently capable of Absoluteness or Limitation. If a free, and not pre-engaged people to any Government, by publick compact yield up themselves to a Person, to be commanded by his Will as their Supream Law, during his Natural Life, and no longer, can it be denyed but that he is an Absolute, and yet Elective Monarch? Unless you will say, he is not Absolute, because he cannot by his Will, as by a Law, bind them to Elect his Son to succeed him, and change their Government into Hereditary. But his being limited in this Clause doth not disparage his Sovereignty, or make his Power of Government limited, because this belongs not to present Government, but is a meer provision for the future. Again, if the power of Ruling according to a Law, be by consent conveyed to one person, and his Heirs to succeed after him, how this should come to be Absolute, and the Entailment should overthrow the Constitution, I cannot imagine: If the whole latitude of power may be by a people made Hereditary, sure a proportion may as well; unless the limitation be such as includes a repugnancy to be perpetual. Indeed this enstating of a Succession makes that power irrevocable; during the continuance of that Succession, but it makes it neither greater nor less in the Successor then was in his Progenitors, from whom he derives it.

Sect. 7. In a successive Monarchy the Successor holds by the Original Right of him who is the Root of Succession; and is *de jure* King the immediate instant after his Predecessors decease: Also the people are bound to him, though they never take any Oath to his Person. For as he Commands in vertue of the Original Right, so they are bound to Obey by vertue of the Original Covenant, and National Contract of Subjection: The New Oath taken either by King or People is but a reviving of the Old; that the Conscience of it by renewing might be the more fresh and vigorous: It neither gives any new Power, nor adds or detracts from the old, unless by common agreement an alteration be made; and so the foundation in that clause is new, which cannot be without the consent of both parties.

CHAP. IV.
Of the Division of Monarchy into Simple and Mixed.

Sect. 1. THE third division is into Simple and Mixed. Simple is when the Government absolute or limited is so intrusted in the hands of one, that all the rest is by deputation from him; so that there is no authority in the whole Body but his, or derived from him: And that One is either individually one person, and then it is a simple Monarchy: Or one associate Body, chosen either

Simple and mixed Monarchy, What?

out of the Nobility, whence the Government is called a simple Aristocracy: or out of the Community, without respect of birth or state, which is termed a simple Democracy. The supreme authority residing exclusively in one of these three, denominates the government simple which ever it be.

Now experience teaching people, that several inconveniences are in each of these, which is avoided by the other: as aptness to Tyranny in simple Monarchy: aptness to destructive Factions in an Aristocracy: and aptness to Confusion and Tumult in a Democracy. As on the contrary, each of them hath some good which the others want, *viz.* Unity and strength in a Monarchy; Counsel and Wisdom in an Aristocracy. Liberty and Respect of common good in a Democracy. Hence the wisdom of men deeply seen in State matters guided them to frame a mixture of all three, uniting them into one Form that so the good of all might be enjoyed, and the evil of them avoided. And this mixture is either equal, when the highest command in a State by the first Constitution of it, is equally seated in all three; and then (if firm Union can be in a mixture of Equality) it can be called by the name of neither of them but by the general stile of a *Mixed State*: or if there be priority of Order in one of the three, (as I think there must be or else there can be no Unity) it may take the name of that which hath the precedency. But the firmer Union is, where one of the three is predominant and in that regard gives the denomination to the whole: So we call it a *Mixed Monarchy*, where the primity of share in the supreme power is one.

What it is which constitutes a mixed monarchy?

Sect. 2. Now I conceive to the constituting of mixed Monarchy (and so proportionately it may be said of the other.)

Pos. 1. The Soveraign power must be originally in all Three, *viz.* If the composition be of all three, so that one must not hold his power from the other, but all equally from the fundamental Constitution: for if the power of one be original, and the other derivative, it is no mixture, for such a derivation of power to others is in the most simple Monarchy: Again, the end of mixture could not be obtained; for why is this mixture framed, but that they might confine each other from exorbitance, which cannot be done by a derivate power, it being unnatural that a derived power should turn back, and set bounds to its own beginning.

Pos. 2. A full equality must not be in the three estates, though they are all sharers in the supreme power; for if it were so, it could not have any ground in it to denominate it a Monarchy, more then an Aristocracy or Democracy.

Pos. 3. A power then must be sought wherewith the Monarch must be invested, which is not so great as to destroy the mixture; nor so titular as to destroy the Monarchy; which I conceive may be in these particulars.

1. If

1. If he be the head and Fountain of the power which governs and executes the established Laws, so that both the other States as well *conjunctim* as *divisim*, be his sworn subjects, and owe obedience to his commands, which are according to established Laws.

2. If he hath a sole or chief power in capacitating and putting those persons or societies in such states and condition, as whereunto such supream power by the foundations of the government doth belong, and is annexed: so that though the Aristocratical and Democratical power which is conjoyned to his, be not from him: yet the definement and determination of it to such persons is from him, by a necessary consecution.

3. If the power of convocating or causing to be put in existence, and dissolving such a Court or Meeting of the two other estates as is authoritative, be in him.

4. If his authority be the last and greatest, though not the sole, which must establish and adde a *consummatum* to every Act. I say these or any of these put into one person makes that State Monarchical, because the other, though they depend not on him *quoad essentiam & actus formales*, but on the prime constitution of the government, yet *quoad existentiam & determinationem ad subjecta*, they do.

The supreme power being either the *Legislative* or the *Gubernative*. In a mixed Monarchy sometimes the mixture is the seat of the *Legislative* power, which is the chief of the two: The power of constituting officers for governing by those Laws being left to the Monarch: Or else the Primacy of both these powers is joyntly in all three: For if the Legislative be in one, then the Monarchy is not mixed but simple, for that is the Superiour, if that be in one, all else must needs be so too: By Legislative, I mean the power of making new Laws if any new be needful to be added to the foundation, and the Authentick power of interpreting the old; For I take it, this is a branch of the Legislative and is as great, and in effect the same power.

Sect. 3. Every mixed Monarchy is limited: but it is not necessary that every limited should be mixed: For the Prince in a mixed Monarchy, were there no definement of him to a Law but only this: that his Legislative acts have no validity without the allowance and joint authority of the other: this is enough to denominate it exactly a limited Monarchy: and so much it must have, if it be mixed. On the other side, if in the foundations of his government he be restrained to any Law besides his own Will, he is a limited Monarch, though that both the Legislative and Gubernative power (provided he exceed not those Laws) be left in his own hands: But then the government is not mixed.

Objection, *As Limitation may be only of the exercise of power, and not of the power it self, so mixture is in regard of persons joined to the Monarch for certain acts and purposes ; but that they should have any share in the Soveraign power, the nature of Monarchy will not admit.*

Answer 1. Just so ; for as a Monarchy is not limited unless there be a limitation of power, for Monarchy is a power: so a Monarchy cannot be mixt unless there be a mixture of powers, for Monarchy is a power ; and to say a mixt Monarchy, and yet the power not mixt, is to speak contradictories.

(2.) If the mixture be not of diverse concurrent powers whereof is it? if you say, of the Monarch and certain other persons joined with him for certain acts and purposes. These joined persons, have they any concurring power to do those acts for which they are joyned if not ; then the adjoyning is futulous and vain, and the power of Monarchy is mixed of a person having power, and of others having no power to do that for which they are joyned. You will say they have power, but not distinct from that of the Monarch: that is, they have none ; for in mixture if it be not distinct, it is none at all. Again if they have any, it must be distinct, for subordinate it cannot be ; if the acts to which they concurre be supream acts, unless we should be so absurd as to say, they may concurre to supream acts, by a subordinate power. But let us see what reason may be urged, for averring a conceit subject to such absurdities.

Such a mixture would make several independant powers in the same state or Kingdom, which is most absurd.

Answer. I grant it is absurd, if you speak of several *complete* independant powers ; but to affirm several incomplete independant powers concurring to make up one *Integral* mixt power, it is no absurdity at all, for so it is in all *Aristocracies* and *Democracies*, and must be acknowledged in all mixed States, where the supremacy is not wholly in the hands of one person. Yet here we do not so make them *independant*, but that we give a large predominancy to one, as, in nature, in all mixed bodies there is ; I grant that it is not necessary the mixture should be so original, but that it may also come afterwards by condescent : It matters not, so it be original, that is, *radical* ; of *Powers*, and not of *meer Acts*. And indeed, there cannot be a mixture of *Acts* unless it be also of *Powers*, for Acts are from Powers ; and where powers are subordinate, there can be no mixture in their acts ; the acts of causes subordinate, are also subordinate, and not co-ordinate and mixed. I have proved that in a mixed government, the concurrents must have independant and distinct powers. (1.) Because, *If the power of one be original and the other derivative, it is no mixture, but a derivation of power which is seen in the most simple Monarchy.*

Objection. But some may say (1.) *That* Derivation *of power is either upon* Substitute Officers *supplying the absence of the Monarch in the execution of power: and this is in the most simple Monarchy. Or else upon persons whose con-*

Chap. 4.   Of Monarchical Government.   23

currence and consent is required to certain acts of Monarchical power; and this makes a mixture, though they have no share in the power it self.

I *Answer*. 1. Absence or Presence of the Monarch; whether they act for him, or with him, varies not the case, if the power they work by be derived from him, then it is his power, and so constitutes no mixture. (2.) As if in the most simple Monarchy the soveraign doth manage the weightiest matters of State alone; and not by consent of his Counsel; without whom he is morally bound, (that is on the sin of rashness) not to transact them, and that is all, which some do yield to the Houses of Parliament, &c. That the King is morally bound to their concurrence and consent in certain Acts. This is nothing but the shaddow of a mixture; if the power of acting be so in one, that if he please, he may do those Acts without the concurrence of these adjunct persons, though he ought not, it is no mixture, because the power is simple and one; and mixed Acts cannot flow frome one simple power. No man of common sense will affirm, that a government can be really mixt and yet the power be simple.

2. Because, *The end of mixture* which is effectual limitation, cannot be had by a derivate power. To which is replyed, though a derivate power cannot set new bounds to the soveraign power, yet may it stand to keep in a legal way those bounds which the soveraign power hath set to it self.

Observe. He dares not say, *they may keep*: but only stand to keep; nor stand neither; but by advice, that is, morally; if he will exceed those bounds, the act is valid, and hath all its authority without them: only he sins if he does so; because he hath promised he will not do it without them: Here is excellent limitation and confinement from exorbitancies: a bare promise without such ado, in constituting *States* and *Mixtures*, would be altogether as good a bounds.

Sect. 4. Now concerning the extent of the Princes power, and the Subjects duty in a mixed Monarchy, almost the same is to be said, which was before in a limited; for it is a general Rule in this matter; such as the Constitution of Government is, such is the Ordinance of God; such as the Ordinance is, such must our Duty of Subjection be. No Power can challenge an obedience beyond its own measure; for if it might, we should destroy all Rules and differences of Government, and make all absolute and at pleasure. In every mixed Principality,

Assert. 1. Look what Power is solely entrusted and committed to the Prince by the Fundamental Constitution of the State, in the due execution thereof all owe full subjection to him, even the other Estates, being but Societies of his Subjects, bound to him by Oath of Allegiance as to their Liege Lord.

How far the Princes power extends in a mixed Monarchy?

Assert.

Assert. 2. Those acts belonging to the power which is stated in a mixed Principle, if either part of that Principle, or two of the three undertake to do them, it is invalid, it is no binding Act; for in this case all three have a free Negative Voice, and take away the priviledge of a Negative Voice; so that in case of refusal the rest have power to do it without the Third, then you destroy that Third, and make him but a Looker on : So that in every mixed Government, I take it, there must be a necessity of concurrence of all three Estates in the production of Acts belonging to that power, which is committed in common to them : Else suppose those Acts valid which are done by any *major* part, that is, any two of the three, then you put it in the power of any two, by a confederacy at pleasure to disannul the third, or suspend all its Acts, and make it a bare Cypher in Government.

Assert. 3. In such a composed State, if the Monarch invade the power of the other two, or run in any course tending to the dissolving of the Constituted Frame, they ought to employ their power in this case to preserve the State from ruine ; yea, that is the very end and fundamental aim in constituting all mixed Policies ; not that they by crossing and jarring should hinder the publick good ; but that, if one exorbitate, the power of restraint and providing for the publick safety, should be in the rest : And the power is put into divers hands, that one should counterpoize and keep even the other : So that for such other Estates, it is not only Lawful to deny Obedience and Submission to Illegal Proceedings, as private Men may, but it is their Duty, and by the foundations of the Government they are bound to prevent dissolution of the Established Frame.

Assert. 4. The Person of the Monarch, even in these mixed Forms, (as I said before in the limited) ought to be above the reach of violence in his utmost exorbitances : For when a people have sworn Allegiance, and invested a Person or Line with Supremacy, they have made it Sacred, and no abuse can devest him of that power, irrevocably communicated. And while he hath power in a mixed Monarchy, he is the Universal Sovereign, even of the other limiting States ; so that being above them, he is *de jure* exempt from any penal hand.

Assert. 5. That one inconvenience must necessarily be in all mixed Governments, which I shewed to be in limited Governments, there can be no Constituted, Legal, Authoritative Judge of the Fundamental Controversies arising betwixt the three Estates. If such do arise, it is the fatal Disease of these Governments, for which no Salve can be prescribed ; for the Established being of such Authority, would *ipso facto* overthrow the Frame, and turn it into Absoluteness : So that if one of these, or two, say their power is invaded, and the Government assaulted by the other, the Accused denying it, it doth become a Controversie : Of this Question there is no Legal Judge; it is a case beyond the possible provision of such a Government. The Accusing side must make it evident to every Mans Conscience. In this case, which is beyond the Government, the Appeal must be to the Community, as if there were no Government; and as by Evidence Mens Consciences are convinced, they are bound to give their utmost assistance. For the intention of the Frame in such States, justifies the exercise of any power, conducing to the safety of the Universality and Government Established.

Of this Particular MONARCHY.

PART II.

CHAP. I.

Whether the Power wherewith our Kings are invested, be an Absolute, or Limited and Moderated Power?

Sect. 1. Having thus far proceeded in general, before we can bring home this to a stating of the great Controversie, which now our sins, Gods displeasure, and evil turbulent men have raised up in our lately most flourishing, but now most unhappy Kingdom. We must first look into the Frame and Composure of our Monarchy; for till we fully are resolved of that, we cannot apply the former general Truths, nor on them ground the resolution of this ruining Contention.

Concerning the Essential Composure of this Government, that it is Monarchical, is by none to be questioned; but the enquiry must be about the Frame of it. And so there are seven great questions to be prosecuted.

Quest. 1. Stated, *Whether it be a Limited Monarchy, or Absolute?* Here the question is not concerning Power in the Exercise, but the Root and being of it; for none will deny but that the way of Government used, and to be used in this Realm, is a designed way: Only some speak as if this definement were an Act of Grace from the Monarchs themselves, being pleased at the Suit, and for the good of the People, to let their Power run into Act through such a course and current of Law; whereas, if they at any time shall think fit on great causes to vary from that way, and use the full extent of their Power, none ought to contradict, or refuse to obey. Neither is it the question, whether they sin against God if they abuse their Power, and run out into acts of injury at pleasure, and violate those Laws which they have by publick Faith and Oath promised to observe; for none will deny this to be true, even in the most Absolute Monarch in the World. But the point controverted is punctually this, *Whether the Authority which is inherent in our Kings be boundless and absolute, or limited and determined, so that the Acts which they do, or command to be done without that compass and bounds, be not only sinful in themselves, but invalid and non-authoritative to others?*

Sect. 2. Now for the determining hereof, I conceive and am in my Judgment perswaded, *that the Sovereignty of our Kings is radically and fundamentally limited,* and not only in the Use and Exercise of it: And am perswaded so on these grounds and Reasons.

Reas. 1. Because the Kings Majesty himself, who best knowes by his Councel the nature of his own Power, says that (a) *the Law is the measure of his Power*; which is as full a concession of the thing as words can express. If it be the measure of it, then his Power is limited by it; for the measure is the limits and bounds of the thing limited. And in his Answer to both the Houses concerning the *Militia,* speaking of the Men named to him, sayes, *If more Power shall be thought fit to be granted to them, then by Law is in the Crown it self, his Majesty holds it reasonable, that the same be by some Law first vested in him, with power to transferr it to these Persons, &c.* In which passage it is granted that the Powers of the Crown are by Law, and that the King hath no more then are Vested in him by Law.

(a) *Declarat. from Newmarket,* Mart. 9. 1641.

Reas. 2. Because it is in the very Constitution of it mixed, as I shall afterwards make it appear, then it is radically limited; for as I shewed before, every mixed Monarchy is limited, though not on the contrary; for the necessary connexion of other Power to it, is one of the greatest limitations. A subordination of Causes doth not ever prove the Supream Cause of limited Vertue; a co-ordination doth alwayes.

Reas. 3. I prove it from the ancient, ordinary, and received denominations; for the Kings Majesty is called our *Liege,* that is, *Legal Sove-*

reign; and we his *Liege*, that is, his *Legal Subjects* : What do these names argue, but that his Sovereignty and our Subjection is Legal, that is, restrained by Law?

Reas. 4. Had we no other proof, yet that of *Prescription* were sufficient : In all Ages, beyond Record, the Laws and Customs of the Kingdom have been the Rule of Government; Liberties have been stood upon, and Grants thereof, with limitations of Royal Power, made and acknowledged by *Magna Charta*, and other publick and solemn Acts; and no Obedience acknowledged to be due but that which is according to Law, nor claimed but under some pretext and title of Law.

Reas. 5. The very Being of our Common and Statute Laws, and our Kings acknowledging themselves bound to govern by them, doth prove and prescribe them limited; for those Laws are not of their sole composing, nor were they Established by their sole Authority, but by the concurrence of the other two Estates; so that to be confined to that which is not meerly their own, is to be in a limited condition.

Some there be which have lately written on this subject, who take another way to prove our Government limited by Law, *viz.* by denying all absolute Government to be Lawful; affirming that absolute Monarchy is not at all Gods Ordinance, and so no Lawful Power secured from Resistance. *Pleaders for defensive Armes, Sect. 2. & 4.* What is their ground for this? God allowes no man to Rule as he list, nor puts mens lives in the pleasure of the Monarch : It is a Power arbitrary and injurious. But I desire those Authors to consider, that in Absolute Monarchy there is not a resignation of Men to any Will or List, but to the *Reasonable Will of the Monarch*, which having the Law of Reason to direct it is kept from injurious Acts. But see for Defence of this Government, Part 1. Cap. 2.

Sect. 3. Having set down those Reasons on which my Judgment is setled on this side, I will consider the main Reasons whereby some have endeavoured to prove this Government to be of an absolute nature, and will shew their invalidity. Many Divines perhaps inconsiderately, perhaps wittingly for self ends, have been of late years strong Pleaders for *Absoluteness* of Monarchical Power in this Land; and pressed Obedience on the Consciences of People in the utmost extremity, which can be due in the most absolute Monarchy in the World; but I seldom or never heard or read them make any difference of Powers, but usually bring their proofs from those Scriptures, where subjection is commanded to the *higher Powers*, and all resistance of them forbidden, and from Examples taken out of the manner of the Government of *Israel* and *Judah*; as if any were so impious to contradict those truths, and they were not as well obeyed in Limited Government as in Absolute; or as if Examples taken out of one Government do alwayes hold in another, unless their aim were to deny all distinction of Governments, and to hold all Absolute, who have any where the Supream Power conveyed to them.

Among these, I wonder most at that late discourse of Dr. *Ferne*, who in my Judgment avoucheth things inconsistent, and evidently contradictory one to the other: For in his Preface he acknowledges our Obedience to be limited and circumscribed by the Laws of the Land, and accordingly to be yielded or denyed to the higher Power; and that *he is as much against an Absolute Power in the King, and to raise him to an Arbitrary way of Government, as against Resistance on the Subjects part*: Also, *that his Power is limited by Law*, Sest. 5. Yet on the other side he affirms, *That the King holds his Crown by Conquest*; that it is *descended to him by three Conquests*, Sect. 2. That we, even our Senate of Parliament hath not so much Plea for Resistance as the antient *Roman* Senate had under the *Roman* Emperors, whose Power we know was Absolute, Sect. 2. That in Monarchy the judgment of many is reduced to one; that Monarchy settles the chief Power and final Judgment in one, Sect. 5. What is this but to confess him Limited, and yet to maintain him Absolute?

Arguments of the contrary disjoined. But let us come to the Arguments. First, say they, our Kings came to their right by Conquest; yea, sayes the Dr. by three Conquests: He means the *Saxons, Danes*, and *Normans*, as appears afterwards: Therefore their Right is absolute. Here, that they may advance themselves, they care not though it be on the ruine of publick Liberty, by bringing a whole Nation into the condition of Conquered Slaves: But to the Argument, 1. Suppose the Antecedent true, the Consequution is not alwayes true; for as is evident before in the first Part; All Conquest doth not put the Conquerour into an Absolute Right. He may come to a Right by Conquest, but not sole Conquest; but a partial, occasioning a Right by final Agreement; and then the Right is specificated by that Fundamental Agreement: Also he may by Sword prosecute a claim of another nature; and in his War intend only an acquiring of that claimed Right, and after Conquest rest in that: Yea farther, he may win a Kingdom meerly by the Sword, and enter on it by Right of Conquest; yet considering that Right of Conquest hath too much of force in it to be safe and permanent; he may think Conquest the best mean of getting a Kingdom, but not of holding, and in wisdom for himself and Posterity, gain the affections of the people by deserting that Title, and taking a new by politick agreement, or descend from that Right by fundamental grants of liberties to the people, and limitations to his own power: But these things I said in effect before, in the first part, only here I have recalled them, to shew what a *non sequitur* there is in the Argument. But that which I chiefly intend, is to shew the infirmity or falshood

of the Antecedent : It is an aſſertion moſt untrue in
to the State : Our Princes profeſs no other way of co
but by right of Succeſſion to Rule free Subjects in a L
the little ſhew of proof theſe Aſſerters have, is from t
So *William* commonly called the Conquerour : For th
an expulſion, not a Conqueſt ; for as our Hiſtories r
into the Kingdom drove out the *Brittains*, and by d
ſelves under their Commanders ; and no doubt contin
had in *Germany* ; unleſs we ſhould think that by conq
own Liberties to the Kings, for whom they conque
Britiſh into *Wales*, Rather I conceive, the Original c
ty was by thoſe our Fore-Fathers brought out of *Ger*
ny : Where, as *Tacitus* reports, *nec Regibus infinita*
libera poteſtas : Their Kings had no abſolute but lim
Power ; and all weighty matters were diſpatched by
neral Meetings of all the Eſtates. Who ſets not here
Liberties and frame of Government ? So they were g
and ſo here to this day, for by tranſplanting themſelve
Soyl, not their Manners and Government : Then, th
indeed a violent Conqueſt ; and, as all violent Rule
when the *Engliſh* expelled them, they recovered their
ties together. Thus it is clear, the *Engliſh* Liberty r
the *Norman* Invaſion, notwithſtanding that *Daniſh* inte
Duke *William*, I know nothing they have in him but t
querour, which ſeems to make for them : The very tr
telligent Reader of the Hiſtory of thoſe times will
William pretended the grant and gift of King *Edward*,
Children, and he came with Forces into this Kingdo
but make good his Title againſt his Enemies ; his end
was not to gain a new abſolute Title, but to vindicate
whereby the Engliſh *Saxon* Kings, his Predeceſſors,
Though his Title was not ſo good as it ſhould be, ye
was better then *Harolds*, who was only the Son of *Go*
wyn, Steward of King *Edwards* houſe ; whereas *Will*
was Couſen to *Emma*, Mother to the ſaid King *Edwa*
by whom he was Adopted, and by ſolemn promiſe c
to ſucceed him : Of which promiſe *Harold* himſelf
bound by Oath to ſee it performed : Here was a fair
gar Atheling the right Heir being of tender age, an
people. Neither did he proceed to a full Conqueſt, b
uſurped the Crown was ſlain in battle, and none to ſucce
being void, the people choſe rather to ſubmit to *William*

that *Harold* by assuming the Crown, provoked the whole Clergy and Ecclesiastical State against him; and we know how potent in those dayes the Clergy were in State affairs: Also that after one Battle fought wherein *Harold* was slain, he went to *London*, was received by the *Londoners*, and solemnly Inaugurated King, as unto whom by his own saying the Kingdom was by Gods Providence appointed, and by vertue of a Gift from his Lord and Cousen King *Edward*, the glorious, granted; so that after that Battle the remainder of the War was dispatched by *English* Forces and Leaders. But suppose he did come in a Conquerour, yet he did not establish the Kingdom on those terms, but on the old Laws, which he retained and authorized for himself and his Successors to govern by. Indeed after his settlement in the Kingdom, some *Norman* Customs he brought in, and to gratifie his Souldiers dispossessed many *English* of their Estates, dealing in it too much like a Conquerour; but the Tryal by Twelve Men, and other Fundamentals of Government, wherein the *English* Freedom consists, he left untouched, which have remained till this day: On the same Title he claimed and was inaugurated, was he King, which was a Title of rightful Succession to *Edward*; therefore he was indeed King not as Conquerour, but as *Edwards* Successor, and on the same right as he and his Predecessors held the Crown. As also by the grant of the former Laws and form of Government, he did equivalently put himself and Successors into the State of Legal Monarchs, and in that Tenure have all the Kings of this Land held the Crown till this day, when these Men would rake up, and put a Title of Conquest upon them, which never was claimed or made use of by him who is the first root of their succession.

    Sect. 4. Another reason which they produce is the successive nature of this Monarchy; for with them, to be Elective and Limited, and to be Successive and Absolute, are equipollent: They conceive it impossible that a Government should be Hereditary and not absolute: But I have enough made it appear, *Part.* 1. *Chap.* 2. *Sect.* 6. That succession doth not prove a Monarchy absolute from limitation, though it proves it absolution from interruption and discontinuance, during the being of that succession to which it is defined. And that which they object that our Kings are actually so before they take the Oath of governing by Law, and so they would be, did they never take that Oath; wherefore it is no Limitation of their Royal power, is there also answered in the next *Sect.* and that so fully that no more need be said. The same Law which gives the King his Crown immediately upon the decease of his Predecessor, conveyes it to him with the same Determinations and Prerogatives annexed, with which his Progenitors enjoyed it, so that he entring on that Original Right, his subjects are bound to yeild Obedience, before they take any Oath: And he is bound to the Laws of the Monarchy before he actually renewes the bond by any Personal Oath. There is yet another argument usually brought to this purpose, taken from the Oath of Allegiance: but of that I shall have occasion to speak hereafter.

CHAP. II.

Quest. 2. *Supposing it be in the Platform limited. Wherein, and how far forth it is limited and defined?*

Pos. 1. I Conceive it fundamentally limited in five particulars. First, In the whole latitude of the *Nomothetical* Power; so that their power extends not to establish any Act, which hath the Being and state of a Law of the Land: nor give an authentick sense to any Law of doubtful and controverted meaning, solely and by themselves, but together with the concurrent Authority of the two other Estates in Parliament.

Pos. 2. In the Governing Power, there is a confinement to the Fundamental Common Laws, and to the superstructive Statute Laws, by the former concurrence of Powers enacted, as to the Rule of all their Acts and Executions.

Pos. 3. In the power of constituting Officers, and means of governing; not in the choice of Persons, for that is intrusted to his Judgment, for ought I know, but in the constitution of Courts of Judicature: For as he cannot Judge by himself or Officers, but in Courts of Justice; so those Courts of Justice must have a constitution by a concurrence of the three Estates: They must have the same power to constitute them, as the Laws which are dispensed in them.

Pos. 4. In the very Succession; for though Succession hath been brought as a *Medium* to prove the Absoluteness of this Government, yet if it be more throughly considered, it is rather a proof of the contrary; and every one who is a Successive Monarch is so far limited in his Power, that he cannot leave it to whom he pleases, but to whom the Fundamental Law concerning that Succession hath designed it. And herein though our Monarchy be not so far limited as that of *France* is said to be, where the King cannot leave it to his Daughter, but to his Heir Male, yet restrained it is; so that should he effect another more, or judge another fitter to succeed, yet he cannot please himself in this, but is limited to the next Heir born, not adopted or denominated; which was the case 'twixt Queen *Mary* and the Lady *Jane*.

Pos. 5. Lastly, In point of Revenue, wherein their Power extendeth not to their Subjects Estates, by Taxes and Impositions to make their own what they please, as hath been acknowledged by *Magna Charta*, and lately by the *Petition of Right*, the case of *Ship-money, Conduct-money, &c.* Nor, as I conceive, to make an Alienation of any Lands, or other Revenues annexed by Law to the Crown. I meddle not with personal limitations, whereby Kings, as well as private men, may limit themselves by Promise and Covenant, which being particular, bind only themselves; but of those which are radical, and have continued during the whole current of succession from unknown times. Other limitations, it is likely, may be produced by those who are skilful in the Laws; but I believe they will be such as are reducible to some of these, which I take to be the principal and most apparent limitations of this Monarchy, and are a most convincing induction to prove my Assertion in the former Chapter, *That this Monarchy, in the very mold and frame of it, is of limited constitution.*

CHAP. III.

Quest. 3. *Whether it be of a Simple or Mixed Constitution?*

Sect. 1. WHen the Government is simple, when mixed; also where the mixture must be, which denominates a mixed Government, is explained *Part.* 1. *Cap.* 3. Now I conceive it a clear and undoubted Truth, that the Authority of this Land is of a compounded and mixed nature in the very root and constitution thereof. And my judgment is established on these grounds.

Answer to the 19 *Propos.*   *Reas.* 1. It is acknowledged to be a Monarchy mixed with Aristocracy in the House of Peers, and Democracy in the House of Commons. Now (as before was made appear in the first Part) it is no mixture which is not in the Root and Supremacy of Power; for though it have a subordination of inferiour Officers, and though the Powers inferiour be seated in a mixed Subject, yet that makes it not a mixed Government; for it is compatible to the simplest in the World, to have subordinate mixtures.

Reas.

is the state of this Monarchy, as appears in the former question, and is self-apparent.

Reas. 3 That Monarchy, in which three Estates are constituted, to the end that the power of one should moderate and restrain from excess the power of the other, is mixed in the root and essence of it ; but such is this, as is confessed in the answer to the said Propositions. The truth of the *major* will appear, if we consider how many ways provision may be made in a Political Frame to remedy and restrain the excesses of Monarchy. I can imagine but three wayes. First, by constituting a legal power above it, that it may be regulated thereby, as by an over-ruling power : Thus we must not conceive of our two Houses of Parliament, as if they could remedy the exorbitances of the Prince by an Authority superiour to his, for this were to subordinate him to the two Houses, to set a superiour above the Sovereign, that is, to destroy the being of his Monarchical Power. Secondly, by an original conveyance to him of a Limited and Legal Power, so that beyond it he can do no Potestative Act ; yet constituting no formal Legal Power to restrain or redress his possible exorbitances ; here is limitation without mixture of another constituted power : As the former of these overthrowes the power of the Sovereign, so this makes no provision for the indemnity of the People. Thirdly, now the never enough to be admired Wisdom of the Architects and Contrivers of the Frame of Government in this Realm (who ever they were) have found a third way, by which they have conserved the Sovereignty of the Prince ; and also made an excellent provision for the Peoples freedom, by constituting two Estates of Men, who are for their condition Subjects, and yet have that interest in the Government, that they can both moderate and redress the Excesses and Illegalities of the Royal Power, which (I say) cannot be done, but by a mixture, that is, by putting into their hands a power to meddle in acts of the highest function of Government ; a power not depending on his Will, but radically their own, and so sufficient to moderate the Sovereigns Power.

Sect. 2. Now what can reasonably be said in opposition to these grounds, proving a fundamental mixture, I cannot devise. Neither indeed is a mixture in the Government denyed by the greatest Patrons of irresistibility ; only such a mixture they would fain make it, which might have no power of positive resistance. I will therefore set down what they probably may or do object to this purpose, and will shew the invalidity thereof.

Object. 1. This mixture seems not to be of distinct Powers, but of a Power and a Councel; Authority in the Prince to give power to Acts, and Counsel in the two Houses to advise and propose wholesome Acts; as if the Royal Power alone did give life to the Law; only he is defined in this power, that he cannot animate any Act to the being of a Law, but such as is proposed unto him by this great and Legislative Councel of Parliament. *Sol.* This were probable, supposing the Parliament were only in the nature of a Councel; but we know it is also a Court, the *High Court of Parliament*: Now it is evident, that a Court is the seat and subject of Authority and Power, and not barely of Counsel and Advice.

Object. 2. The two Houses together with the King, are the Supream Court of the Kingdom; but taken divisely from the King, it is no Court, and consequently hath no power. *Sol.* Suppose them no entire Court divided from the King, yet they are two Estates of the three which make up the Supream Court, so that they have a power and authority, though not compleat and sufficing to perfect an Act, without the concourse of the third: For it appears by the Acts of that Court, that every of the three Estates hath a Legislative power in it; every Act being Enacted by the Kings most Excellent Majesty, and by the *Authority of the Lords and Commons assembled in Parliament.*

Sect. 3. *Object.* 3. They have an Authority, but in subordination to the King, and derived from him, as his Parliament. Indeed this is a main Question, and hath very weighty Arguments on both sides, viz. *Whether the Authority of both the Houses be a subordinate Authority, and derived from the King, as its original?* Three Reasons seem strong for the affirmative:

Whether the Authority of the two Houses be derived from the King?

First, Because it is his Parliament, so called and acknowledged: If his Court, then the power whereby they are a Court is his power, derived from him, as the power of other Courts is. Secondly, Because he hath the power of Calling and Dissolving it. Thirdly, Because he is acknowledged in the Oaths of Allegiance and Supremacy to be the Head, and of Supream Authority in the Kingdom, and all subject to him.

Treatise entituled, A fuller Answer to Dr. Ferne.

And whereas some make Answer, that he is *Singulis major*, but *Universis minor*, so the Answerer to Doctor *Ferne*, I wonder that the Proposition of the Observator, that the King is *Universis minor*, should be so much exploded. Every Member *seorsim* is a Subject, but all *collectim* in their Houses are not: And he sayes simply, the Houses are co-ordinate to the King, not subordinate; that the Lords stile, *Comites,* or *Peeres,* implyes in Parlia-

Chap. 3.   *Of this particular Monarchy.*   35

ment a co-ordinative fociety with his Majefty in the Government. I conceive this Anfwerer to avoid one extream falls on another; for this is a very overthrow of all Monarchy, and to reduce all Government to Democracy; for look where the *apex poteftatis* is, there is the Government. Alfo it is againft common Reafon : For the King, is he not King of the Kingdom? And what is the Kingdom but all united ? All the particulars knit together in one body politick ; fo that if he be King of the Kingdom, he is *Univerfis major* too ; for the King is *major*, and the Kingdom is the united Univerfe of the People. Thus thofe expreffions are fome of them falfe, fome though *fecundum quid* true ; yet fpoken fimply, and in that manner, are fcandalous and incompatible to Monarchy. Thus you fee what may be faid on the one fide, to prove the King to be the original of all Power, even of that which is in the Houfes of Parliament affembled.

On the other fide are as weighty Arguments to prove the contrary, *viz.* That the two Houfes Authority is not dependent, nor derived from the Royal Power. Firft, The Authority of the Houfes being Legiflative, is the Supream, and fo cannot be derived. Three concurrent Powers producing one Supream Act, as *con caufa*, joint caufes of the fame higheft effect cannot have a fubordination among themfelves in refpect of that caufality ; it not being imaginable how a power can caufe the fupream effect, and yet be a fubordinate and derived power. Secondly, The end of conftituting thefe two Eftates being the limiting and preventing the exceffes of the third, their power muft not be totally dependent and derived from the third, for then it were unfuitable for the end for which it was ordained : For to limit an Agent by a power fubordinate and depending on himfelf, is all one as to leave him at large without any limitation at all. Thirdly, That which hath been fpoken of a mixed Monarchy, doth fully prove that the two other powers which concur with the Monarch, to conftitute the mixture, muft not be altogether fubordinate to it, and derived from it. I muft profefs thefe Reafons to prevail with me, that I cannot conceive how the Authority of the two Houfes can in the whole being of it, be a dependant and derived power.

Sect. 4. That we may find out the truth amidft this potent contradiction of both fides, recourfe muft be had to the Architecture of this Government, whereof I muft declare my felf to be fo great an Admirer, that what ever more then Humane Wifdom had the contriving of it, whether done at once, or by degrees found out and perfected, I conceive it unparalleld for the exactnefs of true policy in the whole World ; fuch a care for the Sovereignty of the Monarch, fuch a provifion for the Liberty of the People, and that one may be juftly allayed, and yet confift without impeachment of the other, that I wonder how our Forefathers in thofe rude unpolifhed times could attain

Refolution of the Queftion.

such an accurate Composure. First, Then suppose a people, either compelled to it by Conquest, or agreeing to it by free consent, Nobles and Commons set over themselves by publick compact one Sovereign, and resign up themselves to him and his Heirs, to be governed by such and such Fundamental Lawes: There's a Supremacy of Power set up, though limited to one course of exercise. Secondly, Then because in all Governments after cases will come, requiring an addition of Lawes, suppose them Covenanting with their Sovereign, that if cause be to constitute any other Laws, he shall not by his sole power do that work, but they reserve at first, or afterwards it is granted them, (which is all one) a hand of concurrence therein, that they will be bound by no Laws, but what they joyn with him in the making of. Thirdly, Because though the Nobles may personally convene, yet the Commons (being so many) cannot well come together by themselves to the doing of such a work, it be also agreed that every Corporation of the Commons shall have power to depute one or more to be for the whole in this publick legislative business; that so the Nobles by themselves, the Commons by their Deputies assembling, there may be representatively the whole Body, having Commission to execute that reserved Authority for establishing new Laws. Fourthly, Because the occasion and need of making new Laws, and authentick expounding the old, would not be constant and perpetual, and it would carry an appearance of a Government in which were three Heads and chief Powers, they did not stablish these Estates to be constantly existent, but occasionally, as the causes for which they were ordained should emerge and happen to be. Fifthly, Because a Monarchy was intended, and therefore a Supremacy of Power (as far as possible) must be reserved for one; it was concluded that these two Estates should be Assemblies of his Subjects, sworn to him, and all former Laws; the new, which by agreement of Powers should be Enacted, were to be his Laws, and they bound to obey him in them as soon as established: And being supposed that he who was to govern by the Laws, and for the furtherance of whose Government the new Laws were to be made, should best understand when there was need, and the Assembling and Dissolving the two Estates meeting, was a power of great priviledge, it was put into the Princes hand by Writ to convocate and bring to existence, and to adjourn and dismiss such Meetings. Sixthly, In process of time Princes not caring much to have their Government looked into, or to have any power in act but their own, took advantage of this power of convocating those Estates, and did more seldom then need required make use of it; whereon provision was made, and a time set within which an Assembly of Parliament was to be had. Now when you have made these suppositions in your mind, you have the very model and platform of this Monarchy, and we shall easily find what to answer to the Arguments before produced on either side.

fide. For firſt it is his Parliament, becauſe an Aſſembly of his ſubjects, convocated by his Writ, to be his Councel, to aſſiſt him in making Laws for him to govern by: yet not his, as other Courts are altogether deriving their whole authority from the fulneſs which is in him. Alſo his power of aſſembling and diſſolving proves him thus far above them, becauſe in their exiſtence they depend on him; but their power and authority *quoad ſpecificationem*, the being and kind of it, is from original conſtitution: for they expect no Commiſſion and authority from him, more then for their meeting and reducing into exiſtence; but exiſting they work according to the priviledges of their conſtitution, their acts proceeding from their conjunct authority with the Kings, not from its ſubordination to the Kings. The Oath of Allegiance binds them, and reſpects them as his ſubjects, to obey him, governing according to eſtabliſhed Laws: it ſuppoſes and is built upon the foundations of this Government, and muſt not be interpreted to overthrow them: he is thereby acknowledged to be ſupreme ſo far as to rule them by Laws already made; not ſo far as to make Laws without them, ſo that it is no derogation to their power; and I beleive of theſe things none can make any queſtion. Therein conſiſts the accurate Judgment of the Contrivers of this Form they have given ſo much into the hands of the ſoveraign, as to make him truly a Monarch; and they have reſerved ſo much in the hands of the two Eſtates, as to enable them to preſerve their own liberty.

CHAP. IV.

Queſt. 4. How farre forth it is mixed; and what Parts of the Power are referred to a mixed Principle?

I Shall be the breifer in this, becauſe an anſwer to it may be eaſily collected out of the precedent Queſtions: for he who knows how farre this Government is limited, will ſoon diſcern how far it is mixed, for the Limitation is moſtly affected by the mixture: but diſtinctly, I conceive that there are three parts of the power referred to *Three points of* the joint concourſe of all three Eſtates: So that either of them *Mixture.* not conſenting or ſuſpending its influence the reſt cannot reduce that power ordinarily and legally into act.

1. The firſt is the Nomothetical power, underſtanding by it the power of making, and authentick expounding Laws. So that I believe an act cannot have the nature and form of a Law of the Land, if it proceed from any one, or two of theſe, without the poſitive concurrence of the third.

Se-

Secondly, The power of impoſing taxes and payments on mens eſtates: that the King by himſelf cannot aſſume mens properties by requiring impoſitions not granted him by Law, is often confeſſed: And that the other Eſtates cannot do it by themſelves, I conceive it as unqueſtionable: For it were ſtrange to give that to the ſecondary and aſſiſting powers, which is denyed to the Soveraign and principal. If it be objected that every Corporation electing Deputies, and authorizing them to be *vice totius Communitatis*, do thereby grant them power, and entruſt them as to make laws to bind them, ſo to diſpoſe of any part of their eſtate, either by rate or payment for the publick good: I anſwer, that they are by that deputation enabled as for one, ſo for the other; that is, according to the fundamental uſuage of the Kingdom; that is by the joynt conſent of the other ſtates, for though the Houſe of Commons is choſen by the people, and they repreſent the people, yet the repreſentation doth not give them a power which was not in the people. Now the people have no power to do an act which either directly, or by conſequence doth put it in the will and pleaſure of any one or two of the Eſtates, to overthrow the other: But this power of opening and ſhutting the Purſe of the Kingdom is ſuch a power, that if it be in one or two of the Eſtates, without the third, then they by that power might neceſſitate that other to do any act, or diſable it from its own defence. This and the Legiſlative power have ſuch a neerneſs, that they cannot be divided, but muſt be in the ſame ſubject: this is ſo great a power, that put it abſolutely in any Eſtate ſingle, you make that Eſtate in effect abſolute, making the reſt dependant and beholding to it for their ſubſiſtance.

Thirdly, the power of diſpatching the affairs of the Kingdom which are of greateſt difficulty and weight, the *ardua regni*, which the Writ for convocating the other Eſtates doth mention, ſuppoſing thereby that ſuch difficulties are not to be diſpatched by the power of one alone; for if they were, why then are the two other convocated to be aſſiſting? I acknowledge many matters of great moment may be done by the Regal power, and in ſuch caſe it may be ſaid, that the other Eſtates are gathered *ad melius tranſigendum*, that the adviſe and ſenſe of the Community may be for direction. But I conceive there be two ſorts of affairs, which ought not to be tranſacted without the concurrence of all three. Firſt ſuch as concern the publick ſafety and weal, ſo far as ſtable detriment or advantage comes to the whole body by the well or ill carriage thereof; for then there is the ſame reaſon as in making new Laws: For why was not the power of making any new Laws left in the hands of one, but reſerved for the concurrence of all three? ſave becauſe the end of the Architects was, that no new thing which was of ſo much concernment as the ſtable good and dammage of the Kingdom, ſhould be introduced without the conſent and advice of the whole: ſo that if any buſineſs be of that moment, that it is equipollent to a Law in the publick intereſt,

interest, it should be managed by such an authority and way as that is. Secondly such as introduce a necessity of publick charge, be it matter of War or else, if to the effecting of it the purse of the Kingdom be required, it is evident that it out to be done by the concurrence of all, because they only jointly (as appears before) have power to impose a publick charge on the estates of men. And it were all one to put the power of our estates in the hands of one, as to put the power of such undertakings in his sole hands, which of necessity bring after them an engagement of publick expence.

CHAP. V.

Quest. 5. *How far forth the Two Estates may Oppose and Resist the Will of the Monarch?*

Sect. 1. THis Question is in the general already handled in the first part, so that it will be easie to draw those Answers there to this particular here: Therefore conformably to what I then affirmed, I will answer this Question by divers Positions.

Pos. 1. The Monarch working according to his power, not exceeding the Authority which God and the Laws have conferred on him, is no way to be opposed either by any or all his Subjects, but in conscience to Gods ordinance obeyed. This is granted on all sides.

Pos. 2. If the Will and Command of the Monarch exceed the limits of the Law, it ought for the avoidance of scandal and offence be submitted to, so it be not contrary to Gods Law, nor bring with it such an evil to our selves, or the publick, that we cannot be accessary to it by obeying. This also will find no opposition. Disobedience in light cases, in which we are not bound; makes an appearance of slighting the power, and is a disrespect to the person of the Magistrate. Therefore Christ, to avoid such offence would pay tribute, though he tells *Peter*, he was free, and need not have done it.

Pos. 3. If he command a thing which the Law gives him no authority to command, and it be such as would be inconvenient to obey, in this case obedience may lawfully be denied: This also finds allowance from them which stand most for Royal power. Doctor *Ferne* in his Preface acknowledges obedience to be limited and circumscribed by the established Laws of the Land, and accordingly to be yielded or denied. And *Sect.* 1. says he, *We may and ought to deny obedience to such Commands of the Prince as are unlawful by the Law of God, yea by the established Laws of the Land.* Here he says
more

more then we fay; yea more then fhould be faid, as appears in the fecond Pofition: it is not univerfally true, that we ought.

Pofition 4. If he exceed the limits of the Law, and proceed in courfes illegal, means there are which it is agreed upon the Subjects may ufe to reduce him to legal Government; fo much Doctor *Ferne* allows *Sect.* 4. Cries to God, Petition to the Prince, Denial of Obedience, Denial of Subfidy, &c.

Pof. 5. But the point in controverfie is about pofitive and forcible refiftance, the lawfulnefs of which fome do utterly deny, and others do as confidently maintain: but yet this point might be brought to a narrower ftate then in the confufed handling of it, it ufually is: by diftinguifhing 'twixt forceable refiftance ufed againft the Kings own perfon, or againft inferiour Officers and Inftruments advifing to, or executing the illegal commands.

Sect. 2. For the firft, as I have before expreffed my felf, force ought not to be ufed againft the perfon of the Soveraign, on any pretence whatever by any or all his fubjects; even in limited and mixed Monarchies: for if they be truly Monarchs, they are irrevocably invefted with Soveraignty, which fets their perfons above all lawful power and force. Alfo the Soveraign power being fo conferred on that perfon: The perfon and power cannot be really fundred, but the force which is ufed to the one, muft alfo violate the other: for power is not in the Soveraign as it is in inferiour Officers: as water is otherwife in the fpring then in the channels, and pipes deriving it: It is not infeperably in them, and therefore they offending, force may be ufed againft them without violation of the Ordinance of Authority. Thefe Arguments prove it unlawful in any: That which the Dr. brings, I approve as ftrong againft all private force; where he allows defence againft the perfon of the Prince himfelf, fo farre as to ward his blows, but not to return blows; no though for natural defence: becaufe the Common Wealth is concerned in his perfon, *Sect.* 2. And to divert a private evil by inducing a publick, is unjuft and unlawful: fo that for this point of force againft the perfon of the Prince: I think there ought to be no contention. If any have been fo rafh to hold it lawful on thefe grounds, that the whole Kingdom is above him becaufe they make him King, and that by mifcarriage he may make a forfeiture, and fo lay himfelf open to force: I do judge thefe grounds very infufficient: unlefs the Kingdom referve a fuperiority to it felf, or there be a fundamental claufe of forfeiture on fpecified caufes; and then it is not properly a Monarchy: but all this hath been already handled in the general part.

Secondly, For Inftruments of oppreffion of publick liberty if the wrong be deftructive, and no other means of prevention, but force, be left: I am perfwaded it may be ufed, and pofitive refiftance made againft them; And if I find any contradiction from the moft rigid Patrons of Royalty, it muft be only

Chap. 5. *Of this particular Monarchy.* 41

in this point. And here I muſt complain of the indiſtinct dealing of that Doctor in this matter; who mingleth both theſe points together; and ſcarce ſpeaks any thing to reſolve Mens Conſciences in this: But ſpeaks either in general, or elſe of force againſt the Princes own perſon: Whereas I think, the caſe which ſticks moſt on the Conſcience at this time, is this latter: Of oppoſing, miſ-leading and miſ-imployed Subjects, which he ſpeaks very little to. Nay, he ſeems to me, after all his diſclaiming of reſiſtance, to come home to us, and though ſparingly, yet to aſſent to lawfulneſs of reſiſtance in this point. For *Sect.* 2. ſpeaking of *Davids* guard of armed men: He ſayes, It was to ſecure his perſon againſt the cut-throats of *Saul*, if ſent to take away his life: He means to ſecure it by force, for Souldiers are for force: He means no negative ſecuring by flight, for that may be done even againſt *Saul* himſelf; but he ſpeaks of ſuch a ſecuring which might only be againſt cut-throats. So then he grants ſecuring by force againſt theſe: But they went on *Sauls* Command, and moſtly with his preſence. Again, in the inſtance of *Eliſha*, he ſeems to acknowledge lawfulneſs of perſonal defence againſt the ſudden and illegal aſſaults of Meſſengers, he means by force, for he ſpeaks of ſuch which he will not allow in publick, which can be underſtood of none but by force: But it appears the Doctor in his whole diſcourſe hath avoided this point of reſiſtance of miſ-imployed Subjects; which yet is the alone point which would have given ſatisfaction; for before it appears we agree in all the reſt, and in this too for ought I know, he having not diſtinctly ſaid any thing againſt it.

Sect. 3. Now concerning this caſe of forceable reſiſtance of inferiour perſons miſ-imployed to ſerve the illegal deſtructive commands of the Prince, I will do two things. 1. I will maintain my *Aſſertion* by convincing Arguments. 2. I will ſhew the invalidity of what is ſaid againſt it.

W ether reſiſtance of Inſtruments of will be lawful?

Aſſert. 1. This then is my *Aſſertion*: The two Eſtates in Parliament may lawfully by force of Armes reſiſt any perſons or number of perſons adviſing or aſſiſting the King in the performance of a Command illegal and deſtructive to themſelves, or the publick.

Arg. 1. Becauſe that force is lawful to be uſed for the publick conſervation, which is no reſiſtance of the Ordinance of God; for that is the Reaſon condemning the reſiſtance of the Powers: Now this is no reſiſtance of Gods Ordinance: For by it neither the perſon of the Sovereign is reſiſted, nor his power: Not his perſon, for we ſpeak of Agents imployed, not of his own perſon: Nor his power; for the meaſure of that, in our Government, is acknowledged to be the Law: And therefore he cannot confer Authority to any beyond Law; ſo that thoſe Agents deriving no Authority from him, are meer Inſtruments of his Will: Unauthorized perſons; in their aſſaults Robbers, and as Dr. *Ferne* calls them, Cut-throats. If the case be put, What if the Sovereign himself in person be present with such Assaylants, joining his personal assistance in the execution of his Commands? It is much to be lamented, that the will of the Prince should be so impetuous in any subverting Act, as to hazard his own person in the prosecution of it. Yet supposing such a case, all counsels and courses must be taken, that no violence be offered to his person, and profession of none intended: But no reason the presence of his person should priviledge ruining Instruments from suppression, and give them an immunity to spoil and destroy Subjects to better themselves: His person being secured from wrong, his power cannot be violated in such an Act, in which none of it can be confered on the Agents. And sure *David*, though he avoided laying hands or using any violence against the person of *Saul*, and on no extremity would have done it: Yet for the Cut-throats about him, if no other means would have secured him, he would have rescued himself by force from their outrage: Though *Saul* was in their company: Else what intended he by all that force of Souldiers, and his enquiry of God at *Keilah*; by which it is plain, he had an intent to have kept the place by force, if the people would have stuck to him: Neither is it to the purpose which the Dr. sayes, *Sect*. 2. That his example was extraordinary, because he was anointed and designed to succeed *Saul*, for that being but a designation, did not exempt him from the duty of subjection for the present, or lessen it, as is plain by the great Conscience he made of not touching *Saul*: But he knew it was one thing to violate *Sauls* person and power, and another to resist those Instruments of Tyranny, the Cut-throats which were about him.

Arg. 2. Because without such power of resistance in the hands of Subjects, all distinction and limitation of Government is vain; and all forms resolve into Absolute and Arbitrary; for that is so, which is unlimited; and that is unlimited, not only which hath no limits set; but also which hath no sufficient limits; for to be restrained from doing what I will, by a power which can restrain me no longer nor otherwise then I will, is all one, as if I were left at my own Will. I take this to be clear: Now it is as clear, that without this forceable resistance of Instruments of usurped power be lawful, no sufficient limits can be to the Princes Will, and all Laws bounding him a e to no purpose. This appears by enumerating the other means, Prayer to God, Petition to the Prince, Denyal of Obedience, Denyal of Subsidy: A moderate use of the power of denying, as Dr. *Ferne* calls it: These are all; but what are these to hinder, if a Prince be minded to overthrow all, and bring the whole Government to his own Will? For Prayer, and Petition, these are put in to fill up the number: They are no limitations, they may be used in the most absolute Monarchy; for denyal of Obedience, that may keep me from being an Instrument of publick servitude; but Princes Wills never want them which will yield obedience, if I deny it; yea enough to destroy all the rest, if nothing be left them but to suffer: Then for denyal of Subsidy, if he may by thousands of Instruments take all, or what he, or they please, and I must not resist; what need he care whether the people deny or grant : If a Prince be taught that he may do it, Cases and Reasons will soon be brought to perswade him, that in them he may Lawfully do it ; as late experiences have given us too much Testimony : Thus it is apparent, that the denyal of this power of resistance of Instruments overthrows and makes invalid all Government, but that which is absolute; and reduces the whole world *de jure* to an absolute subjection, that is, servitude : For the end of all constitution of moderated forms is not that the supream power might not lawfully exorbitate, but that it might have no power to exorbitate.

The Dr. is conscious hereof ; and therefore tells us in his *Sect.* 5. This is the very reason which is made for the Popes power of curbing and deposing Kings in case of Heresie ; because else the Church, sayes the *Papist*, hath no means for the maintenance of the Catholick Faith, and its own safety : But who sees not the vast difference 'twixt these two ? And that the same reason may be concluding here, which is apparently *non* concluding there : For 1. They thereby would draw to the *Pope* an authoritative power ; we no such superiour power ; but only a power of resistance for self-conservation, which Nature and the Law of Reason gives to every one; and may stand with the condition of subjection and inferiority. 2. They on this reason give the *Pope* a power over the very person of the King; we only of resisting of unauthorized invading destroyers, coming under the colour of an Authority, which is not in the Sovereign to be derived. 3. They prove a civil right for Spiritual Reasons, we only for Civil Reasons. 4. The Church and the Faith are constituted in their very formal being from Christ himself, who is the Head and great Shepherd immediately in his own person; and as it is his own Family, so he keeps the power of preserving it in his own hands; having made direct and particular promises to assure us of their upholding against all subversion by his own power ; so that here is assurance enough without visible means of force for a Spiritual Body which lives by Faith. But in a Civil State there is no such assurance nor supporting promises : Power only in the undefined being of it being Gods immediate Ordinance, and not in this specificated or determinate being ; wherefore it hath no such immediate provision made for its preservation, no promise of a divine power for its standing ; but as it is left by God to Mens Wisdom to contrive the frame, so to their Providence to establish means of preservation. As the Body is outward and civil, so the upholding means must be such ; Spiritual and infallibly assuring a formed State hath not, as the Church and Faith have ; if there be none of outward force and power neither, then none at all it hath, and is in ill case indeed. But there is an art full of venome, when a truth cannot be beaten down by juſt reaſoning, then to make it odious by hateful compariſons ; ſo in this caſe aſperſions are caſt, as if the Patrons of Reſiſtance did borrow the Popiſh and Jeſuitical grounds, and their Poſitions as dangerous to Kings, as the Jeſuits Hell-bred and bloody Principles : Whereas it appears by all this diſcourſe, and I am perſwaded is written in Capital Letters in the very Conſcience of them which deſpitefully object it, that there is no congruity at all 'twixt their Doctrines, no more then 'twixt Light and Darkneſs.

Arg. 3. Becauſe ſuch power is due to a publick State for its preſervation, as is due to a particular perſon : But every particular perſon may lawfully by force reſiſt illegal deſtructive Miniſters, though ſent by the command of a legal Sovereign, provided no other means of ſelf-preſervation be enough. This Aſſumption the Doctor ſeems to grant ; he denies it to be lawful againſt the perſon of the Prince, but in effect yields it againſt ſubordinate perſons : But the main is againſt the Propoſition, and the Doctor is ſo heavy a friend to the State, that he thinks it not fit to allow it that liberty he gives every private man. But whoſe Judgment will concur with his herein, I cannot Imagine ; for ſure the Reaſon is greater, the publick ſafety being far more precious, and able to ſatisfie the dammages of a publick reſiſtance, then one particular mans is of a private. But of this more in anſwer to his Reaſons.

Arg. 4. Becauſe it is a power put into the two Eſtates by the very reaſon of their Inſtitution ; and therefore they not only may, but alſo ought to uſe it for publick ſafety ; yea they ſhould betray the very truſt repoſed in them by the Fundamentals of the Kingdom if they ſhould not. An Authority Legiſlative they have : Now to make Laws and to preſerve Laws are acts of the ſame power ; yea, if three powers jointly have intereſt in making of Laws, ſurely either of theſe ſeverally have, and ought to uſe that power in preſerving them. Alſo that the Authority which the Houſes have is as well given them for preſerving the Government by Eſtabliſhed Laws, as for eſtabliſhment of Laws to govern by, is a truth proved by the conſtant uſe of their power to that end, in correcting the exorbitance of inferiour Courts, queſtioning delinquent Judges and Officers of State for violations, and much is done in this kind by the ſole Authority of the Houſes, without the concurrence or expectance of Royal Power ; ſo then, ſuppoſing they have ſuch an Authority for ſafety of publick Government, to queſtion and cenſure inferiour Officers for tranſgreſſions, though pretending the Kings Authority, can it be denyed but that their Authority will bear them out to uſe forcible reſiſtance againſt ſuch, be they more or fewer.

Arg. 5. The Kings Warrant under his hand exempts not a Malefactor from the cenſure of a Court of Juſtice, nor puniſhment impoſed by Law, but the Judge muſt proceed againſt him according to Law ; for the Law is
the

the Kings publick and authoritative Will ; but a private Warrant to do an unlawful act, is his private and unauthoritative Will : wherefore the Judge ought to take no notice of such Warrant, but to deal with the offender as no other then a private man. This proves that such Instruments thus illegally warranted, are not authorized ; and therefore their violence may be by force resisted, as the assaults of private men, by any ; and then much rather by the Houses of Parliament : which supposing them divided from the King to have no complete authority, yet sure they have two parts of the greatest Legislative authority. But I fear I shall seem superfluous, in producing Arguments to prove so clear a truth : Is it credible that any one will maintain so abject an esteem of their authority, that it will not extend to resistance of private men, who should endeavour the subversion of the whole frame of Government, on no other Warrant then the Kings Will and pleasure ? Must they be meerly passive ? Is patience, and the denial of their Votes to a subversion, all the opposition they must use, if a King (which God forbid) should on his Royal pleasure send Cut-throats to destroy them as they sit in their Houses ? Is all their authority (if the King desert them or worse) no more then to petition, and suffer ; and by a moderate use of their power of denying, dissent from being willing to be destroyed ? If power of resisting by force of subverters armed by the Kings Will (for by his Authority they cannot) be unlawful for them, all these absurdities must follow : yea, the vilest Instrument of Oppression, shewing but a Warrant from the King to bear him out, may range and rage all his dayes through a Kingdom, to waste and spoil, tax and destrain, and at utmost of his insolence must have no more done to him by the Parliament it self, then to stay his hand, as the basest Servant may his Masters, or the meanest subject the Kings own hand ; by the Doctors own confession. Consider then and admire, if any men of Learning will deny this power of forcible resistance of Ministers, of subverting commands to be lawful. I have thus far confirmed my assertion, not that I find any openly opposing it, but because the Doctor and some other seem to have a mind that way, and do strike at it, though not professedly and in open dispute.

For the several proofs brought in behalf of resistance, some of them prove as much as is here asserted ; others are not to the purpose. Particularly, that of the peoples rescuing *Jonathan* from his Fathers bloudy resolution proves lawfulness of hindering unreasonable self-destructive purposes, even in absolute Monarchies, if it prove any thing. That of *Uzzah*'s thrusting out by the Priests, is not to the purpose : but *Davids* raising and keeping Force about him, and his purpose at *Keilah*, proves the point directly, *viz*. Lawfulness of forcible resistance of Cut-throats, even though *Saul* himself were in presence : This the Doctor sees plainly, and therefore shuffles it off, by saying, *His example is extraordinary* ; as if he were not a present Subject because he was designed by Gods revealed counsel to be a future King. And he confesses *Elisha*'s example of shutting the door against the Kings messenger proves personal defense against sudden illegal assaults of Messengers, which is the thing in Question.

Arguments on the contrary dissolved.
Sect. 4. Let us now view the strength of what is said against resistance whether any thing comes home against this Assertion. The Doctors proofs from the Old Testament come not to the matter: *Moses*, and afterwards the Kings, were of Gods particular designation, setting them absolutely over the people, on no condition or limitation; so that did they prove any thing, yet they concern not us, respecting a Government of another nature. But particularly, that of *Corah* and the Princes rebelling against *Moses*, is not to the matter; it was a resistance of *Moses* own Person and Office; and doubtless penury of other proofs caused this and the rest here to be alledged: For that 1 *Sam.* 8. 18. how inconsequent is it, to say, the people should cry unto the Lord, therefore they had no other means to help them but cries to God; though (I confess) in that Monarchy they had not. That speech 1 *Sam.* 26. 9. was most true there, and is as true here, but not to the purpose, being spoken of the Kings own person. But the main authority brought against resistance, is that *Rom.* 13. and on that Doctor *Ferne* builds his whole discourse: Let us therefore something more largely consider what is deduced out of that Text. First he supposes the King to be the *Supream* in Saint *Peter*, and the *Higher Power* in Saint *Paul*. Secondly, he collects *All Persons*, every soul is forbidden to resist. Thirdly, that then was a standing Senate, which not long before had the supream power in the Roman State: It is confessed; but that they could challenge more at that time when Saint *Paul* writ, then our great Councel will or can, I deny: For that State devolving into Monarchy by Conquest, they were brought under an Absolute Monarchy, the Senate it self swearing full subjection to the Prince; his Edicts and Acts of Will were Laws, and the Senates consent only *pro forma*, and at pleasure required. He who reads *Tacitus* cannot but see the Senate brought to a condition of basest servitude, and all Laws and Lives depending on the will of the Prince: I wonder then the Doctor should make such a Parallel. Indeed the Senate had been far more then ever our Parliaments were or ought to be: but now that was far lesse then our Parliament hath been, or (I hope) ever will be: They were become the sworn Vassals of an absolute Emperour, ours the sworn Subjects of a Leige or Legal Prince. Fourthly, he says, then was more cause of resistance, when Kings were Enemies to Religion, and had overthrown Laws and Liberties. I answer, There were no causes for Resistance: Not their enmity to Religion had they but legal power, because Religion then was no part of the Laws, and so its violation no subversion of established government. And for the overthrow

of

Chap. 5.   *Of this particular Monarchy.*   47

of Laws and Liberties, that was paſt and done, and the government new, the Senate and all the reſt actually ſworn to abſolute Principality: Now an Ordinance of abſolute Monarchy was conſtituted, the ſacred bond of an Oath had made it inviolate. But what would he inferre hence, all being granted him? Sure this he doth intend, That every ſoul among us, ſeveral, and conjoyned in a Senate, muſt be ſubject for conſcience, muſt not reſiſt, under pain of Damnation: All this, and whatever beſides he can juſtly infer out of that Text, we readily grant: But can any living man hence collect, that therefore no reſiſtance may be made to fellow-ſubjects, executing deſtructive illegal acts of the Princes will in a legal Monarchy? Will he affirm that the Ordinance of God is reſiſted, and Damnation incurred thereby? Gods Ordinance is the power, and the perſon inveſted with that power; but here force is offered to neither as before I have made it appear. And herein we have B. *Biſſon* conſenting, where he ſays, that *the ſuperiour power here forbidden to be reſiſted, is not the Princes will againſt his Laws but agreeing with his Laws*. B. *of ſubject* I think the day it ſelf is *p. 94. and 220.* not more clear then this ſatisfaction, to all that can be concluded out of that Text: ſo the foundation of all that diſcourſe is taken from it, if his intent were thence to prove unlawfulneſs of reſiſtance of Inſtruments of Arbitrarineſs in this Kingdom.

Let us alſo conſider the force of his reaſons, whether they impugne this point in hand. He ſays, ſuch power of reſiſtance would be no fit means of ſafety to a State, but prove a remedy worſe then the diſeaſe His Reaſons, firſt becauſe it doth tend to the overthrow of that order, which is the Life of a Common-wealth, it would open a way to People, upon the like pretences, to reſiſt, and even overthrow power duly adminiſtred. 2 It may proceed to a change of government. 3. It is accompanied with the evils of Civil-War. 4. On the ſame ground the two Houſes proceed againſt the King, may the people proceed to reſiſtance againſt them; accuſing them not to diſcharge their truſt. Laſtly, ſeeing ſome muſt be truſted in every State. It is reaſon the higheſt and final truſt, ſhould be in the higheſt power. Theſe are his main reaſons on which he builds his concluſion againſt reſiſtance.

To his firſt, I ſay it were ſtrange if reſiſtance of diſtructive diſorder ſhould tend to the overthrow of Order: It may for the time diſturb, as Phyſick while it is in working diſturbs the natural body, if the peccant humors make ſtrong oppoſition: but ſure it tends to health, and ſo doth this reſiſtance of diſorder to Order. Neither would it open a way for the people to violate the Powers; for doing right can open no way to the doing of wrong, If any wicked ſeditious ſpirits ſhould make uſe of the Vail of Juſtice to cover unnatural Rebellion: Shall a peoples right and liberty be taken from them to prevent ſuch poſſible abuſe? Rather let the foulneſs of ſuch pretences diſcover it ſelf, ſo God and good men will abhorre them: ſuch Cloakes of Rebellion have in former Ages been taken off, and the Authours brought to juſt confuſion, without the expence of the liberties of this Kingdom.

To the ſecond, muſt not inſtruments be reſiſted, which actually intend, and ſeeked a change of Government: becauſe ſuch reſiſtance may proceed to a change of government? Is not an unlikely poſſibility of change to be hazarded, rather then a certain one ſuffered? But I ſay, it cannot proceed to a change of government, unleſs it exceed the meaſure of lawful reſiſtance: yea it is impoſſible, that reſiſtance of inſtruments ſhould ever proceed to a change of government; for that includeth the greateſt reſiſtance and violation of the perſon and power of the Monarch, the lawfulneſs of which I utterly diſclaim.

Thirdly, it is not ever accompanied with the evils of Civil War: But when the Princes Will finds enough inſtrument of their Countreys ruine to raiſe it. And then the miſchief of that War muſt light on thoſe which raiſe it. But ſuppoſe it may enſue, yet a temporary evil of war is to be choſen rather then a perpetual loſs of liberty, and ſubverſion of the eſtabliſhed frame of a government.

In the fourth, I deny the parity of reaſon: for the two Houſes are bodies conſtituted and endowed with Legiſlative authority, and truſt of preſervation of the frame, by the Fundamentals of the Kingdom: which the people out of thoſe Houſes are not. Again the government being compoſed of a threefold conſenting power, one to reſtrain the exorbitance of another: All three together are abſolute and equivalent to the power of the moſt abſolute Monarch: The concurrent Will of all three, makes a Law, and ſo it is the Kingdoms Law. And to the laſt,

I anſwer, In every State ſome muſt be truſted, and the higheſt truſt is in him who hath the Supream power: theſe two, the ſupream Truſt, and the Supream power are inſeperable: and ſuch as the power is, ſuch is the truſt: An abſolute power ſuppoſes an abſolute truſt: A power allayed with the annexion of another power as here it is ſuppoſeth a truſt of the ſame nature. A Joint truſt, yet ſaving the ſupremacy of the Monarch, ſo far forth as it may be ſaved, and not be abſolute, and the others authority nullified.

How far forth the ſword is in the hand of the Monarch. It may be further argued, that it being the Prerogative Royal to have the managing of the ſword, that is, Legal force in the Kingdom; none can, on any pretence whatever, uſe lawful force, either againſt him, or any, but by his Will: for it is committed to him by law, and to none but whom he aſſigns it to: ſo that the Laws of the Kingdom putting all power of force and Arms into his truſt, have placed him, and all thoſe who ſerve him, in a ſtate of irreſiſtibleneſs in reſpect of any lawful force. This is a point much ſtood on and on this ground, the Parliament now aſſuming the diſpoſing of the *Militia* by an Ordinance, it is complained on, as a uſurping of what the Law hath committed to the

Chap. 5.   *Of this particular Monarchy.*   49

King, as his Prerogative: The opposing of which Ordinance by a Commission of *Array*, was the beginning of this miserable Civil War. I will distinctly lay down my Answer hereto, submitting it to every impartial judgment.

Pos. 1. The power of the Sword being for defence of the Laws, by punishing violaters, and protecting Subjects; it is subservient to Government, and must needs belong to him who is entrusted with the Government, as a necessary requisite, without which he cannot perform his trust.

Pos. 2. As it is an appendix to the power of Government, and goes along with it, so it goes under the same terms; belonging to the Prince, as the other doth; *sc.* Absolutely, to use at will where the Monarchy is absolute; or with limitation, to use according to Law, where the Monarchy is limited; so that in this Government the Armes and Sword of the Kingdom is the Kings, to a defined use committed to him; *viz.* For defence of the Laws and Frame of Government established, and not for Arbitrary purposes, or to enable Ministers to execute commands of meer Will.

Pos. 3. The two Houses in vertue of the Legislative Authority, in part residing in them, are interested in the preservation of Laws and Government, as well as the King: And in case the King should misimploy that power of Arms to strengthen subverting Instruments: Or in case the Laws and Government be in apparent danger, the King refusing to use the Sword to that end of preservation for which it was committed to him: I say, in this case, the two Estates may by extraordinary and temporary Ordinance assume those Armes wherewith the King is entrusted, and perform the Kings trust: And though such Ordinance of theirs is not formally Legal, yet it is eminently Legal, justified by the very intent of the Architects of the Government, when for these uses they committed the Armes to the King. And no doubt they may command the strength of the Kingdom to save the being of the Kingdom; for none can reasonably imagine the Architectonical Powers, when they committed the power of Government and Armes to one to preserve the Frame they had composed, did thereby intend to disable any, much less the two Estates, from preserving it, in case the King should fail to do it in this last need. And thus doing the Kings work, it ought to be interpreted as done by his Will; because as the Law is his Will, so that the Law should be preserved is his Will, which he expressed when he undertook the Government: 'Tis his deliberate Will, and ought to be done, though at any time he oppose by an after Will, for that is his sudden Will, as Dr. *Ferne* himself *Sect.* 1. doth teach us to distinguish.

I know some do say, *if by these mis-imployed Persons be understood the Commanders and Souldiers of the Kings Armies, they cannot see (nor any man else they think) but that the resisting of them by a contrary Militia, is a resisting of the King, and unlawful?*

H   *Answ.*

Anfw. I cannot see, nor any man else, I think, why Commanders and Souldiers should have a priviledge of subverting States and Governments more than other men: Can the Royal Power extend to give them an irresistability, and not to others? Certes, if others may be resisted, much rather Commanders and Souldiers, because there is greater danger of subversion from them than from others: Their being Commanders and Souldiers makes them more dangerous, but not more priviledged.

Object. *If they come with pretence of Authority, there may be seeking redressment above from Authority, but if that may not be had, yet no resistance.*

And who then minding to kill or rob, may not make a pretence of Authority, that so he may effect his mischief without repugnance.

Object. *The Ministers of Power in each County, and the Houses of Parliament also, may at first stay, restrain, and commit such mis-imployed Instruments, and so represent the matter again to the King, this is not to resist.*

Anfw. If mis-imployed Instruments may be stayed, restrained and imprisoned, sure they may be resisted: Else what if they should choose, and will not be committed; the Parliament must not lay hands on them to compel them; for so there may chance to be fight and slaughter in the apprehension, and then it will be (I think) called resistance.

Object. *But suppose the Houses of Parliament do commit such Persons, and represent the matter to the King, and the King should be so obstinate as to persist in the maintenance of those illegal courses, and to that end employ the Militia, it is neither Legal nor Reasonable they should pursue the Opposition to the setting up a contrary Militia or Power.*

Anfw. Here we see the upshot of the *English* freedom, and priviledge of Parliament: This is that destroys all Policies, reducing them all to that which is Arbitrary: If the King should set Souldiers to destroy Laws and Parliaments, they may (if they be able) stay their hands till they go to the King, and know whether it be indeed his Will and Pleasure to have them destroyed or no; if he say yea; then they must return and submit to the vilest Instruments of subversion, and not lift up a hand to resist them.

Object. *It will be said what I plead for, is a contestation of Power with him whose Ministers they are, a levying of War, and opposing of Armies against Armies.*

Anfw. Sure these men do much abhor a Civil War; I cannot blame them; but yet we may buy an immunity too dear, at the price of a subversion of Religion, Laws and Government, which is the case in dispute. This were to choose to be kill'd rather then to fight; to have a State subverted, rather than disturbed by a War to prevent it. I grant, there must be no contestation of Power with him whose Ministers they are; but this is the point to be proved, that in this case it is so: I utterly deny the

Royal

Royal Power in our State can be communicated to subverting Instruments; and I do in vain expect, while they prove that which every where they suppose; for they build all on this foundation, *viz. That Gods Ordinance is an absolute unlimited Power, investing the whole Will of the Supream, and cannot be determined in the exercise, but only morally.* The vanity of which conceit will appear hereafter. In this place I note only, that while men pretend a detestation of Civil War, they can do nothing more to foment it, than by defending such positions of intollerable Servitude : Did not such rigid *Courfellors* of the *King of Israel* cause the greatest *rent* and *Civil War* that ever was made in any Kingdom.

But some throw upon us the state and practice of *Christ, that he resisted not*, &c. *Matth.* 10. 25.

Answ. What? Is every Christian bound for his outward state to be in no better case then Christ was? If he were pleased to be born under an Absolute Government, to be of low and poor Condition, doth this impose a necessity on all to be no freer, no richer than he was? Let it be proved that by the Providence of God we are brought forth under such a Government as our *Master* was, then will we hold our selves bound by his Example, to abide quietly in that Condition we are born to; but if God, as he hath dispensed to many a richer Estate then Christ was pleased to have, so hath he to us a freer Government; then the Apostle adviseth us *to use it rather*, and not to be trifled out of it, by a shew of our Masters Example, in a case in which it binds no man.

Object. But you are altogether failing in express Scripture; your Faith and Perswasion is only resolved into an appearance of Reason.

Answ: Mr. *Hooker* will teach you, that the intent of Scripture is to deliver us *credenda*; but in matters within the compass of Reason, it is enough if we have evident Reason for it, *Scriptura non contradicente :* And I am confident the Scripture hath not a tittle against such a resistance as I do maintain, and hath as much for it as a matter of that nature need to have; and we have reason enough for it.

The Question with us in *England* is, *Whether in a limited Monarchy, Resistance of subversive Instruments be unlawful?* Some affirm what I deny. Some undertake to satisfie Mens Consciences that it is unlawful; bringing not one Text of Scripture, which speaks to the point. On the other side, we have both to settle Mens Consciences; on (1.) Example of Scripture, &c. The Peoples rescue of *Jonathan, Davids* arming against the Cut-throats of *Saul*, that is, subversive Instruments; these being *particular men*, and in an *absolute Monarchy*, prove the point the more strongly; so strongly that Dr. *Ferne* is fain to fly to that ordinary evasion of an *extraordinary Priviledge*. Besides all those places which prove it lawful to resist private men, seeking to subvert Laws and Religion, and the publick good, sith in a limited State they are but private men, though backt with a Commiſſion from the Kings Will and Pleaſure. (2.) Then for Reaſon; I am confident the meaneſt apprehenſion (from what is ſaid in this Chapter) will diſcern, that they who make the Monarchs ſole Will the laſt Judge of all Controverſies; and ſimply deny in the laſt caſe of ſubverſion, all power of reſiſtance of Inſtrumeuts, even to the Supream Courts of Law and Juſtice; do without any Controverſie, reſolve all Government into an Arbitrary Abſoluteneſs. They allow indeed a kind of diſtinction of Monarchies, but all within the compaſs of *Abſolute* : *A legal reſtraint* they ſeem to acknowledge; but ſuch a one as reſolves into the Arbitrary Will of the Monarch.

Architectonical Powers. I find one diſpleaſed thereat: Why ſo ? *This is the Riddle of this Governing Power originally in the People, they are Architectonical Powers, but built upon foundations laid in the Air:* For this Reaſon, For before Government eſtabliſhed they have not any politick Power, whereby a Command may be laid upon others, but only a natural Power of private Reſiſtance. This is falſe that they have *only* a natural Power of private Reſiſtance. They have indeed no formal politick Power, for we ſpeak of a People free from all Government; but they have a vertual, radical Power, by publick Conſent and Contract to conſtitute this or that form of Government, and reſign up themſelves to a condition of ſubjection on *Terms*, and after a form of their own conſtitution; ſo the *Athenians, Lacedimonians,* and *Romans* of old having expelled their Kings; and the *United Provinces* with others of later times have done : This is what is called *Architectonical Power.*

Objection, Then it is not the denyal of Reſiſtance which makes a Monarch Abſolute, but the denyal of a Law to bound his Will; I do grant it ? But withal I ſay, that it is *neceſſario conſequentivum*, though it be not *conſtitutivum :* For ſith a Monarch which is Abſolute hath no Law to bound his Will; but his very Will is the Subjects Law; then every act of his Will is Gods Ordinance, and ſo by conſequence it is unreſiſtable.

CHAP. VI.

Queſt. 6. *In what caſes the other Eſtates may, without or againſt the Kings Perſonal Conſent, aſſume the Armes of the Kingdom ?*

Sect. 1. WHoever were the Authors of that Book lately Publiſhed, ſtiled, *Scripture and Reaſon pleaded for defenſive Armes,* have laid new and over-large grounds for Reſiſtance. Two Aſſertions

Chap. 6.   *Of this particular Monarchy.*   53

they endeavour to maintain : Firſt, *Thoſe Governours (whether Supream or others) who under pretence of Authority from Gods Ordinance, diſturb the quiet and peaceable life in Godlineſs and Honeſty, are far from being Gods Ordinance in ſo doing,* Sect. 3. Secondly, *This Tyranny not being Gods Ordinance, they which reſiſt it even with Armes, reſiſt not the Ordinance of God.* Hereon, Sect 4. they free Chriſtians, even in the Apoſtles time, and ſo under the Roman Emperours, or any other Government, from neceſſity of paſſive ſubjection in caſe of perſecution; affirming, that the Chriſtians in thoſe firſt perſecutions, had they been ſtrong enough, might have uſed Armes for defence againſt the Tyranny of their Emperours. Their ground is from the Reaſons uſed by the Apoſtle, *Rom.* 13. where he commands ſubjection, and forbids reſiſtance to the higher power, becauſe *they are Gods Ordinance, his Miniſters for praiſe to well-doers, for terror to evil-doers.* But I muſt profeſs my ſelf to diſſent from them in this opinion, conceiving that the Apoſtle in urging thoſe Reaſons drawn from the due ends of power, doth intend to preſs them to ſubjection by ſhewing them what benefit comes to Men by Authority in its due uſe; and not to ſhew them how far they are bound to be ſubject, and in what caſes they may reſiſt : For had he ſuch a meaning at that time, when the Governours did altogether croſs thoſe ends of their Ordination, he had taught them rather a Doctrine of Reſiſtance then Subjection ; ſhall we conceive that he would preſs ſubjection to Powers in the hands of Heathens and Perſecutors, if he had not intended they ſhould paſſively be ſubject unto them, even under thoſe Perſecutions? Rather I approve the received Doctrine of the Saints in antient and modern times, who could never find this licenſe in that place of the Apoſtle ; and do concur with Maſter *Burroughs*, profeſſing againſt Reſiſtance of Authority, though abuſed : *If thoſe (ſayes he) who have power to make Laws, make ſinful Laws, and ſo give Authority to any to force Obedience, we ſay here there muſt be either flying, or paſſive Obedience.* And again, *We acknowledge we muſt not reſiſt for Religion, if the Laws of the Land be againſt it.* But what do they ſay againſt this? In making ſuch Laws againſt Religion the Magiſtrates are not Gods Ordinance ; and therefore to reſiſt is not to reſiſt Gods Ordinance : As an inferiour Magiſtrate, who hath a Commiſſion of Power for ſuch ends, is reſiſtable if he exceed his Commiſſion, and abuſe his Power for other ends ; ſo Princes being Gods Miniſters, and having a deputed Commiſſion from him to ſuch ends, *viz.* the promotion of Godlineſs, Peace, Juſtice, if they pervert their power to contrary ends may be reſiſted without violation of Gods Ordinance. That I may give a ſatisfactory Anſwer to this, which is the ſum of their long Diſcourſe, I muſt lay it down in ſeveral Aſſertions.

Whether it be lawful to take up Armes againſt the Magiſtrate perverting his power to a wrong end?

Anſwer to Dr.Fe ne Sect. 2,

Assert. 1. I acknowledge Gods Ordinance is not only power, but power for such ends, *sc.* the good of the People.

Assert. 2. It is also Gods Ordinance, that there should be in men, by publick consent called thereto, and invested therein, a power to choose the means, the Laws and Rules of Government conducing to that end; and a power of Judging in relation to those Laws, who be the well doers which ought to be praised, and who the evil doers who ought to be punished. This is as fully Gods Ordinance as the former; for without this the other cannot be performed

Assert. 3. When they who have this final civil Judicature shall censure good men as evil doers; or establish iniquity by a Law to the encouragement of evil doers; in this case, if it be a subordinate Magistrate doth it, appeal must be made (as St. *Paul* did) to the Supream; if it be the Supream which through mistake or corruption doth mis-censure, from whom there lyes no Civil Appeal, then without resistance of that Judgment we must passively submit: And he who in his own knowledge of innocency or goodness of his cause shall by force resist, that man erects a Tribunal in his own heart against the Magistrates Tribunal; clears himself by a private Judgment against a publick, and executes his own sentence by force against the Magistrates sentence, which he hath repealed and made void in his own heart. In unjust Censures by the highest Magistrate, from whom there is no Appeal but to God, the sentence cannot be opposed till God reverse it, to whom we have appealed: In the mean time we must suffer as Christ did, notwithstanding his Appeal, 1 *Pet.* 2. 23. and so must we notwithstanding our Appeal, 1 *Pet.* 4. 19. for he did so for our example. If an Appeal to God, or a censure in the Judgment of the condemned might give him power of resistance, none would be guilty, or submit to the Magistrates censure any further then they please. I desire those Authors, before they settle their judgment in such grounds (which I fear will bring too much scandal) to weigh these particulars. First, Their opinion takes away from the Magistrate the chief part of Gods Ordinance, *sc.* power of definitive judgment of Laws and Persons, who are the good, and who the bad, to be held so in civil proceedings. Secondly, They justifie the Conscience of Papists, Hereticks, and grossest Malefactors to resist the Magistrate, in case they be perswaded their cause is good. Thirdly, They draw men off from the commands of patience under persecution, and conforming to Christ and his Apostles, in their patient enduring without verbal or real opposition, though Christ could not have wanted power to have done it, as he tells *Peter*. Fourthly, They deprive the Primitive and Modern Martyrs of the glory of suffering, imputing it either to their ignorance or disability. Fifthly, It is a wonder, that sith in Christ and his Apostles time there was so much use of this power of resistance, they would by no express word shew the
Christians

Christians this liberty, but condemn resistance so severely. Sixthly, There is in the case of the Parliament now taking up Armes no need of these offensive grounds; Religion being now a part of our National Law, and cannot suffer but the Law must suffer with it.

Sect. 2. Now to the proposed Question I answer, first Negatively, *sc.* 1. It ought not to be done against all illegal proceedings, but such which are subversive and unsufferable. Secondly, Not publick resistance, but in excesses inducing publick evils; for to repel private injuries of highest nature with publick hazzard and disturbance, will not quit cost, unless in a private case the common Liberty be struck at. Thirdly; Not when the Government is actually subverted, and a new form (though never so injuriously) set up, and the People already engaged in an Oath of absolute subjection; for the remedy comes too late, and the establishment of the new makes the former irrevocable by any justifiable power, within the compass of that Oath of God: This was the case of the Senate of *Rome* in Saint *Pauls* time. Secondly, Affirmatively: I conceive three cases when the other Estates may lawfully assume the force of the Kingdom, the King not joyning or dissenting, though the same be by Law committed to him. First, When there is Invasion actually made, or imminently feared by a Forreign Power. Secondly, When by an intestine Faction the Laws and Frame of Government are secretly undermined, or openly assaulted: In both these cases the Being of the Government being endangered, their trust binds, as to assist the King in securing, so to secure it by themselves, the King refusing. In extream necessities the liberty of Voices cannot take place, neither ought a *Negative Voice* to hinder in this exigence, there being no freedom of deliberation and choice, when the Question is about the last end: Their assuming the Sword in these cases is for the King, whose Being (as King) depends on the Being of the Kingdom; and being interpretatively his act, is no disparagement of his Prerogative. Thirdly, In case the Fundamental Rights of either of the three Estates be invaded by one or both the rest, the wronged may lawfully assume force for its own defence; because else it were not free, but dependant on the pleasure of the other. Also the suppression of either of them, or the diminishing of their Fundamental Rights, carries with it the dissolution of the Government: And therefore those grounds which justifie force to preserve its Being, allows this case, which is a direct innovation of its Being and Frame.

_{1 *When Armes ought not to be assumed.*}

_{2. *When they may be assumed.*}

CHAP. VII.

Quest. 7. *Where the Legal Power of Final judging in these cases doth reside, in case the Three Estates differ about the same?*

The Question Stated.

Sect. 1. IN this Question (for our more distinct proceeding) some things are necessarily to be observed. First, that we meddle not here with the judicature of Questions of inferiour nature; *viz.* such as are 'twixt subject and subject, or the King and a subject, in matter of particular right, which may be decided other way, without detriment of the publick Frame, or diminution of the priviledges of either of the three Estates. Secondly, difference is to be made even in the Questions of outmost danger: First, for it may be alledged to be either from without, by invasion of forraign Enemies; or by a confederacy or intestine subverters in which neither of the three Estates are alledged to be interessed, and so the case may be judged without relation to either of them, or detriment to their priviledges. Here I conceive a greater latitude of power may be given to some to judge without the other; for it inferrs not a subordinating of any of the three to the other. Secondly, or else it may be alledged by one or two of the Estates against the other, that not contenting it self with the powers allowed to it by the Laws of the government, it seeks to swallow up, or entrench on the priviledges of the other, either by immediate endeavours, or else by protecting and interessing it self in the subversive plots of other men. Thirdly, in this case we must also distinguish betwixt, first, authority of raising Forces for defence against such subversion, being known and evident: secondly, and authority of judging and final determining, that the accused Estate is guilty of such design and endeavour of subversion, when it is denied and protested against. This last is the particular in this Question to be considered; not whether the people are bound to obey the authority of two, or one of the Legislative Estates in resisting the subversive assaies of the other, being apparent and self-evident; which I take in this Treatise to be clear. But when such plea of subversion is more obscure and questionable, which of the three Estates hath the power of ultime and supream judicature by Vote or sentence to determine it against the other; so that the people are bound to rest in that determination, and accordingly to give their assistance, *eo nomine*, because it is by such power so noted and declared?

Determination of the question.

For my part in so great a cause if my earnest desire of publique good and peace, may justifie me to deliver my mind, I will prescribe to the very Question: for it includes a solecism in government of a mixt temperature: To demand which E-

Chap. 7.   *Of this particular Monarchy.*   57

state may challenge this power of final determination of Fundamental controversies arising betwixt them, is to demand which of them shall be absolute: For I conceive that in the first part hereof, I have made it good, that this final utmost controversie arising betwixt the three Legiflative Estates, can have no legal, constituted Judge in a mixed government: for in such difference, he who affirms that the people are bound to follow the Judgement of the King against that of the Parliament, destroys the mixture into absoluteness: And he who affirms that they are bound to cleave to the Judgment of the two Houses against that of the King, resolves the Monarchy into an Aristocracy, or Democracy, according as he places this final Judgement. Whereas I take it to be an evident truth, that in a mixed government, no power is to be attributed to either Estate, which directly, or by necessary consequence, destroys the liberty of the other.

Sect. 2. Yet it is strange to see, how in this Epidemical division of the Kingdom, the Abettors of both parts claim this unconcessible Judgment. But let us leave both sides, pleading for that which we can grant neither, and weigh the strength of their Arguments.

First, Dr. *Ferne* lays down two Reasons, why this final Judgment should belong to the King. 1. Monarchy, says he, *Sect.* 5. settles the chief power and final Judgment in one. This *Position* of his can be absolutely true no where but in absolute Monarchies: and in effect his book knows no other then absolute government. 2. Seeing some one must be trusted in every State, *It is reason*, says he, *Sect.* 5. *the highest and final trust, should be in the higher and Supream power*. I presume by final trust, he means the trust of determining these Supream and final disagreements; and accordingly I answer; It is not necessary that any one be trusted with a binding power of Judicature in these cases; for by the foundations of this government, none is, yea, none can be trusted with it: for to intend a mixed government, and yet to settle the last resolution of all judgment in one, is to contradict their very intention. Neither in a constituted government must we dispose of powers according to the guesse of our reason; for mens apprehensions are various; the Dr. thinks this power fittest for the King: His answerers judge it fittest for the two Houses, and give their reasons for it too. Powers must there reside, where they are *de facto* by the Architects of a government placed: he who can bring a fundamental Act stating this power in any, says something to the matter: but to give our conjectures, where it should be, is but to provide fuel for contention.

Dissolution of Arguments placing it in the King.

On the contrary, The Author of that which is called *A Fuller Answer to that Dr.* hath two main Assertions placing this Judgment in the two Houses.

Dissolution of the Arguments placing it in the two Houses.

1. The final and casting result of this States Judgment concerning what
                                    I   these

these Laws, dangers, and means of prevention are, resides in the Two Houses of Parliament, says he, p. 10.

2. In this final resolution of the States Judgment, the people are to rest, *ibid*. p. 14. Good Lord! What extream opposition is between these two sorts of men? If the maintenance of these extreams be the ground of this Warr, then our Kingdom is miserable, and our Government lost which side soever overcome: for I have, more then once, made it good, that these Assertions are destructive on both sides: But I am rather perswaded, that these Officious Propugners overdo their work, and give more to them whose cause they plead, then they ever intended to assume: Nay, rather give to every one their due: give no power to one of these three to crush and undo the other at pleasure: But why doth this Answer give all that to the Two Houses which ere while they would not suffer, when the Judges in the case of Ship money had given it to the King? sure, when they denied it to him, they did not intend it to themselves. 1. He tells us, in them resides the reason of the State: And that the same reason and Judgment of the State which first gave this government its being, and constitution; therefore all the people are to be led by it and submit to it as their publick Reason and Judgment.

I answer, If by state, he mean the whole Kingdom: I say, the reason of the Two Houses divided from the King, is not the reason of the Kingdom, for it is not the Kings reason, who is the head and chief in the Kingdom. If by state be meant the people, then it must be granted, that as farr forth as they represent them, their reason is to be accounted the reason of the Kingdom: and doth bind so far forth as the publique reason of the Kingdom can bind after they have restrained their reason and will to a condition of subjection: so that put case it be the reason of the state, yet not the same which first gave this government its being: for then it was the reason of a State, yet free and to use their reason and Judgment in ordaining a government: but now the reason of a State bound by Oath to a government, and not at liberty to resolve again: Or to assume a supream power of judging, distructive to the frame of government they have established, and restrained themselves unto. Their reason is ours, so far as they are an ordained representative body: But I have before demonstrated, that in this frame, the Houses could not be ordained a legal Tribunal to passe Judgement in this last case: for then the Architects by giving them that Judicature, had subordinated the King to them, and so had constituted no Monarchy. 2. He argues, the Parliament being the Court of supream Judicature and the Kings great and highest Council, therefore that is not to be denied to it, which inferiour Courts ordinarily have power to do, *viz*. To judge matters of right between the King and Subject: Yea, in the highest case of all: The Kings power to tax the subject in case of danger, and his being sole Judge of that danger, was brought to cognizance, and passed by the Judges in the Exchequer. I answer, 1. There is not the same reason betwixt the Parliament and other courts. In these the

King is Judge, the Judges being deputed by him, and judging by his authority; so that if any of his Rights be tryed before them, it is his own Judgment, and he judges himself; and therefore it is fit he should be bound by his own sentence: But in Parliament the King and People are Judges, and that not by an authority derived from him, but originally invested in themselves. So that when the two Estates judge without him in any case not prejudged by him, it cannot be called his Judgment, (as that of the other Courts, being done by his Authority) and if he be bound by any Judgment of the two Estates without him, he is bound by an external power which is not his own; that is, he is subordinated to another power in the State where he is Supream; which is contradictory. Secondly, In other Courts, if any case of right be judged 'twixt him and the Subject, they are cases of particular Rights which diminish not Royalty, if determined against him. Or if they pass cases of general right, (as they did in that of Ship-money) it is but declaratively to shew what is by Law due to one and the other; yet their Judgment is revocable, and lyable to a Repeal by a Superiour Court, as that was by Parliament. But if the Kings Prerogatives should be subjected to the Judgment of the two Estates, the King dissenting then he should be subject to a sentence in the highest Court, and so irremediable; a Judicatory should be set up to determine of his highest Rights without him, from which he could have no remedy. Thus main causes may be alledged, why, though other Courts do judge his Rights, yet the two Estates in Parliament (without him) cannot; and it is from no defect in their power, but rather from the eminency of it, that they cannot. If one deputed by common consent of three, doth by the power they have given them determine Controversies between those three, it is not for either of them to callenge right to judge those cases, because one who is inferiour to them doth it. Indeed if the power of the two Houses were a deputed power, as the power of other Courts is, this Argument were of good strength; but they being concurrents in a Supream Court by a power originally their own, I conceive it hard to put the power of final Judgment in all Controversies 'twixt him and them exclusively, or solely into their hands.

Sect. 3. If it be demanded then how this Cause can be decided? and which way must the People turn in such a contention; I answer, if the non-decision be tolerable, it *What to be done in such a contention?*
must remain undecided, whilst the Principle of Legal decision is thus divided, and by that division each suspends the others power. If it be such as is destructive, and necessitates a determination, this must be made evident; and then every Person must aid that part, which in his best Reason and Judgment stands for publick good, against the destructive. And the Laws and Government which he stands for, and is sworn to, justifies and bears him out in it; yea, binds him to it. If any wonder I should justifie a power in the two Houses to resist, and command aid against any Agents of

deſtructive commands of the King, and yet not allow them power of judging when thoſe Agents or Commands are deſtructive. I anſwer, I do not ſimply deny them power of judging and declaring this; but I deny them to be a Legal Court ordained to judge of this caſe Authoritatively, ſo as to bind all People to receive and reſt in their judgment for Conſcience of its Authority, and becauſe they have Voted it: 'Tis the evidence, not the power of their Votes, muſt bind our Reaſon and Practice in this caſe: We ought to conceive their Votes the Diſcoveries made by the beſt eyes of the Kingdom, and which in likelihood ſhould ſee moſt: But when they Vote a thing againſt the proceedings of the Third and ſupream Eſtate, our Conſciences muſt have evidence of Truth to guide them, and not the ſole authority of Votes; and that for the Reaſon ſo oft alledged.

CHAP. VII.

The Contention now in being is debated, and the readieſt means of Reconcilement Propoſed.

Sect. 1. THus have I (for my own ſatisfaction, and the Conſcience of every moderate and impartial man who will peruſe the ſame) ſet down what I verily conceive to be the truth concerning thoſe high matters, firſt of Monarchy in general, and then of this of *England*, and have given my determination concerning all the weighty Queſtions which ariſe conſiderable in the courſe of handling both: Now nothing remains, but to reſolve the Conſcience by this precedent light, what to judge of the unhappy contention, which now is broken out into open Warre, between the King and the Two Houſes. But this depending on manner of fact, is more fitly referred to every mans own memory and Judgment; and nothing is to be done, but to acquaint himſelf with the certain truth of thoſe matters of fact, and then to judge thereof according to the former Rules. To this iſſue the whole controverſie is brought, *That the Two Houſes may lawfully reſiſt by force of Arms, all Counſels and Attempts of what Men ſoever, tending to the ſubverſion of the eſtabliſhed Frame of Government, or themſelves and their fundamental Priviledges*: which is equivalent to the other: yea though they are warranted by *the commands and perſonal preſence of the King himſelf*: And that clearly this is no reſiſtance of the higher power in our Government, (ſo no force be intended or uſed againſt the Kings own Peeſon) nor doth it come within the cenſure of Saint *Paul Rom.* 13. nor any other Scripture, nor right Reaſon grounded thereon; ſo that the Conſcience aſſured hereof, hath nothing elſe to do but to enquire whether the truth of Fact lyes either in the Affirmative of the Two Houſes; *That the Kingdom was in imminent danger, the King refu-*

sing to join with them for prevention of it, when they assumed the Militia for defence: Or else in the Kings Negative. Much hath been said on both sides, to draw the Consciences of men to adherence; and many (no doubt) have judged according to their pre-ingaged affections: Many papers have I seen running out on both sides to unjustifiable extreams, and have much holpen on the contention, by making the breach wider: yea, I have read more said for them then (I am perswaded, notwithstanding the heat of the contention) either will say for themselves, or can without the subversion of the other.

Sect. 2. Now for a man to resolve his Conscience about the lawfulness or unlawfulness of this War, the course is not to cry it down indefinitely, as a resistance of Gods Ordinance, nor of the higher Power: Nor to justifie it, because the cause stood for, is Religion, and expurgation of in-crept corruptions in Church and State: For all standing for Religion and Reformation is not a justifiable cause to take up Armes; we having proved it before, that in this Kingdom nothing can warrant it, but apparent danger from destructive Counsellors and Instruments. Neither is it enough to demand, as Dr. *Ferne* doth, *Sect. 6. Who were first in Armes?* for the other part will by their Almanack find Armes and Forces gathered and employed before those in *Hull*; but that is not the resolving enquiry; it may fall out the defensive part may be first in Armes, to prevent the ruine of Counsels and ſlots which are apparently contrived, but not executed. The resolving enquiry (I think) must be, *Whether at the Parliaments taking up of Armes, the Commonwealth, Frame of established Government,* or (which is all one) *the Being and radical Powers of Parliament were in apparent danger of subversion?* For if so, then the Armes and Force used against the Counsellors or Agents thereof is proved lawful by all the precedent discourse.

A debate upon the contention.

Declar. of the Lords and Commons of Apr. 3. 1642.

Now it will be alledged, and is in part acknowledged, that there was a grand intention and plot of altering the Government of this Kingdom, and reducing it to an arbitrary way. They will not say his Majesty was conscious of it; but it was aimed at by many about him, and in power with him, whom it concerned to have him absolute: By these men he was told that such things were Law, which if they had been so, then he had been absolute by Law. They will instance in the long and purposed disuse of Parliaments: The arbitrary Taxes and Impositions on most of the Commodities of the Kingdom: The encroachment of the Arbitrary Courts upon the Legal: The Imposition of Ship-money: And the Judges opinion that the King had power to tax the Subject in times of danger, and that he is the sole Judge of that danger: The raising an Army, and forcing the Subject to furnish the same with Coat and Conduct-money. The intention of bringing up the

His Majesties Answ. to the Petit. of the Lords, March 26. 1642.

the Army, to subvert, or at best, to awe and confine the Parliament to bounds of proceeding of their own setting. All this before, or upon the beginning of the Parliament. Then the evidences and proofs against the Earl of *Strafford*, his Majesties coming with the terror of such an attendance into the House of Commons, to demand such a number of Members. Here is a succession of designs, all before the least shew of resistance; for his Majesties coming to the House was *Jan.* 4. 1641. And the first Petition to his Majesty about the *Militia* was not till the 26th of the same: And their resolution to settle it by themselves, his Majesties refusing was not till *March* 1. And among all these there is not one but tends to destroy the frame of Government. Not that every one who had a hand in them did aim at such a destruction; but looking on the design it self (and we must judge of mens intentions by the nature of their Counsels and Enterprizes,) every one of them strikes at the foundation of this Legal Frame, and tends to the introduction of Absoluteness and Arbitrariness in the Sovereign.

I acknowledge that since that time, there is a Plea on both sides of danger of subversion: The King withdrew from *London*, and oft affirms that *He was driven thence*, and could no longer remain in safety: And the two Houses on the former designs plead a danger of subversion from evil Counsellors. Both sides now complain of danger, and have taken up Armes to repel that danger; but these complaints of danger, and taking up of Armes by both sides, was all since the succession of those fore-rected plots. I know what hath been intended or done since the taking of Armes may be all affirmed to be for defence against danger; the withdrawment of so many Members of both Houses, the acts of hostility on both sides, the taxing, spoiling, and undoing of thousands of innocent people, all must be excused by necessity of War, and self-defence. But what can be said for all those Plots and Essaies, which were the Parliaments first grounds of Fears and Forces? Were they removed before they took up Armes, and so their assuming them made causless and inexcusable? You will say, Those were the Plots of Men in Grace and Authority about his Majesty, and that the illegality of those proceedings being made known to him, he disclaims them, professing solemnly he hath no intent but to govern by Law; and acknowledges that the Law is the measure of his power. But they do tell you, That they object nothing against his Majesty, they impute nothing to him, nor use force against him, but those destructive Counsellors, and their Abettors which are about him; because their danger is not from his intentions, but from theirs. It is answered, that his Majesty offers to secure them, the Laws, Liberties, and Religion, by any Acts they shall devise to that purpose. They will tell you, their danger is not from want of Laws to secure them, for they are secured by Law already; their danger is from Men, and their Plots and Designs

Parliament Remonstrance, May 19. 1642.

signs to overthrow Law; and a danger of subversion of Law cannot be secured by Law; succeeding Laws can be no better nor stronger then former Laws; so that where those Men and their Counsels are in power, whose aim hath been the subversion of Parliaments, Liberties and Laws; and those Doctrines remain affirmed and maintained by the Clergy of that side, which subvert all limitations of Monarchy, make all Laws Acts of Grace, and revocable Immunities granted to Subjects; condemning for Rebellion all force used even by the Parliament it self, against the meanest Instruments of violence imployed by the Princes Will; making the Princes Will and Gods Ordinance one and the same thing, of the same latitude; so that resistance of one is resistance of the other; such Counsellors and such Doctrines are (they say) the ground of publick danger, from which no Laws but Justice can secure us. Publick Liberty and Power of forcible resistance of Instruments of servitude are so conjoined, that if you make it unlawful simply to use such power of resistance, you make it unlawful for a People to be free.

Sect. 3. What course then can be sufficient to answer their demands of safety, if Laws cannot do it? Though I incur the censure of high presumption, yet I will be so bold to afford my opinion herein, submitting it to the censure of every Judicious Reader; wishing it were worthy to be scanned by those, in whose hands it is to heal our divisions. What honest heart doth not bleed, to see the ruine of this late flourishing Kingdom go on so fast? Who can do other then speak his mind, who conceives he thinks of any thing which may conduce to Peace, and the re-uniting of this divided Body? Suffer me therefore to disclose my heart in a case, in which every good man hath a deep interest. Thus then I could heartily desire.

Means of reconcilement proposed.

Petit. 1. That the Parliament would desire and seek in this unusual way of Force, no more then what makes necessarily for their, and the publick security; for none can justifie force in them, any further then for security of their Priviledges, Laws, and Frame of Government.

Petit. 2. That his Majesty would be pleased (according to his gracious Resolution, *viz. To deny only those things, the granting whereof would alter the Fundamental Laws, and endanger the foundation on which publick happyness is built:*) to condescend to all Acts of safety, both by establishing of Laws tending to it; and removal of persons of destructive Counsels and Judgments, because the danger alledged is from such.

A sw. to the Petition of Commons, Jan. 28. 1641.

Petit. 3. That because their main fear hath been, that while his Majesty is swayed by such persons, whose judgment and endeavours have been for Absoluteness, the Militia of the Kingdom may be by them (making use of his Majesties Authority) employed in bringing to pass their long fomented, and not yet deserted design; his Majesty would be pleased (for this present) to authorize such over the Militia whom the Houses shall approve of, not thereby disparaging his power over the Militia, which by Law is invested in him; but satisfying by a condescent of grace, their fears from apprehensions of present danger.

Petit. 4. That the two Houses (in their wisdom) would put a difference between those persons who were the antient Delinquents, Contrivers, and principal Agents in the former designs of Arbitrariness; and those Members of both Houses, who since the Kings with-drawnment, and their assuming the Militia, have gone from the Houses to serve and adhere to his Majesty: For since the time that both parts have declared themselves to be in danger, many good Subjects and Patriots have followed the parts, from conscience and perswasion of the truth of Allegations on either side, as their care and opinion of either Party hath lead them; (not that I can acquit them, who on any misleading assist the destructive party from guilt, as Accessaries and Instruments of so unnatural a design) but that I cannot see how the authority and freedom of either of the three Estates can choose but under-go a shew of disparagement, if its adherents and propugners (when it cries out of danger of subversion from the other, and calls and requires their assistance) should be proceeded against and punished as Delinquents, when they profess their aim hath been no more then to preserve the just Rights of any of the Fundamental Estates of the Kingdom, without impairment of the other.

Petit. 5. That if possible, all those might be re-admitted into their several Houses, which are not guilty of the former designs for Absoluteness, and have nothing alledged against them but their adherence to the King in this division, and might sit and act securely there, according to the due freedom of their Houses.

Petit. 6. That his Majesty (for the sake of Peace, and present necessity of composing this distemperature) would be pleased to put himself upon the Judgment and Affection of the two Estates so Assembled in their full Bodies, and suspend the use of his Negative Voice, resolving to give his Royal Assent to what shall pass by the major part of both Houses freely Voting, concerning all matters of grievance and difference now depending in the two Houses. I am confident, if ever this War be transacted without the ruine of one side, which will endanger, if not undo the whole, it must be some such way of remission of rigour on both sides, as I have now described: Which the God of Peace, in whose Hands are the Hearts and Counsels of Men, speedily and graciously effect for his Name sake.

A Vin-

A Vindication of The TREATISE OF MONARCHY:

Containing an Answer to Objections made against it. Also a fuller Discovery of some main Points therein.

Part III.

Chap. I.

Wherein the Vanity and Falshood of the Supposals whereon some do build their Discourses, is made appear.

Sect. 1. Error in the search of Controverted Truths doth more often arise from the *Judgment*, than from the *Reason*: Men do more offend in laying false grounds, than in deducing false inferences from true grounds; so that overthrow their Foundation, and then all their Building will of it self ruine into apparent falshood. The Men of Arbitrary Temper and Principles in this Age go on Supposals, I doubt not to call *unsound* and false; which may be reduced to four heads.

(1.) Concerning the *Ordinance of God in Sovereignty*.
(2.) Concerning the *Nature and Quality of Limitation*.
(3.) The *Means and Causes of Limitation*.
(4.) The *Constitution* of the *English Monarchy*.

(1.) Of the *Ordinance of God in Magistracy*, they proceed on two false Principles:

1. That *the Governing Power is one and the same which God gives and settles upon the Person that is Supream*; that is, it is absolute and unlimited in the Power it self; and may be limited only in the Exercise thereof.

2. Which follows from the former, that *Consent of People* may be the mean of designing the Person, and yielding Subjection to him, who else could not challenge it more than another Man; also a mean of limiting that Power in the exercise of it; but not the measure of the Power it self, which in such a measure is given of God to all Soveraigns, so then let this be the question, Whether it be God's Ordinance that governing Power in all Sovereigns be one unlimited thing; and can receive no measure from the People they affirm it; if they can make it good, in vain do we inquire about the *Constitution* of this Monarchy; or the lawfulness of *Resistance* of Subversive Instruments of the Princes Will. Do they think a Covert *Insinuation* would serve the turn to impose such an Assertion, which frustrate the intent of mankind in framing Limitations of Governing Power; and captives all into an absolute passive subjection to the vilest Instruments of the Will of him who is Supream.

Two main Proofs are given, *Viz.* (1.) *Before Government established, the People have not any Power of a Community, or Politick Power. whereby a Command may be laid upon others; but only a Natural Power of private Resistance.* (2.) *People have not of themselves out of Government, the main Power, the Power of Life and Death, how then can they give it either for Government, or reserve it for Resistance.*

Now I hold the *Negative* of this Question; and doubt not to approve it firm Truth: To that end,

1. I will premise such things as we agree in, that so the point in question may the more distinctly appear; which I apprehend are or may be these.

(1.) That *Governing Power* is Originally from God's Ordinance.

(2.) That it being so, *is unresistable in its whole Latitude, in all the Acts which flow from it.* This the Apostle is clear for, *Rom.* 13. and for no more that I know. Also that this is true, as well in Limited, as Absolute Governments; *V. g.* In Absolute Monarchy, where Authority doth invest the whole Will, the Monarch is unresistable in all the Acts of his
reaso-

reasonable Will; because all are Acts flowing for God's Ordinance. So in Limited Monarchy, where Authority doth not simply invest the Will of a Monarch, but so far forth as it is regulated by such a Law, the Monarch is unresistable in all the Acts of his Will which are according to that Law; because they are Acts flowing from God's Ordinance: Yet though either of these do limit himself in the *Exercise* of his Power, no way thereby diminishing the fullness of his Power; and afterward exceed those Limits, yet he is unresistable, and to be subjected to *actively* in lawful things, and *passively* in unlawful; my reason is, because even those Acts, notwithstanding Limitation, flow from God's Ordinance of Authority which remains the same, and not lestned by such Limitation. (3.) *This Governing Power is Ordinarily conveyed to Persons by publick consent*, which is a point made good in the Treatise. (4.) *That this publick consent is not only a mean, but hath a causal influence in conveying Authority to Persons.* (5.) *That Men working by such consent as second causes, do necessarily convey such Authority, as God hath ordained*; so that if it can be proved either by Scripture or sound Reason, that it is God's Ordinance, that Supremacy should be unlimited, and as large as all the Acts of his Will which hath it, then whatever Men capitulate about Limitation of it, is vain. (6.) *Limitation of Power may be either of Acts*, when Power is conveyed to Persons to do certain Acts of Powers; but not all. Or else of *manner of Working*; when Power is conveyed to do all Acts of Authority, but according to such a prescribed Rule. Now I grant the former cannot be in the Conveyance of Soveraign Power, an inferiour Officer may be limited by Commission to certain Acts of Power; and have no Authority to do other Acts of Power; but when Soveraignty is conveyed, and the Person is set up *next to God above all the People*, he must have an unlimited Power, in respect of Acts of Government; for God's Ordinance is not only that there should be Power for such an end; *sc. a peaceable Life in Godliness and honesty*; but *sufficiency of Power* for the attainment of that end: So that all Power of doing any Act needful for that end, must be in him who is Supream, and the Comprehensive Head of Power to Inferiour Magistrates. So that all the question truly stated is about the other sort of Limitation, *sc. Whether Soveraign Power be so unlimited in its Rule of Acting, that it investeth the whole reasonable Will of him who hath it:* So that all the Acts which proceed from him who hath it according to the Rule of his own Reason, be *potestative*, and from God's Ordinance. Secondly, Having thus punctually stated the Question, the Determination must proceed in a double way, *sc.* (1.) In *Simple* Government. (2.) In *mixed* Governments. I do maintain the Negative in both; and my proofs shall be formed accordingly. *Assert.* 1. Then in *Simple Government, Power is not one unlimited thing in the Supream:* But may be limited in the very being and root of it: As these following Reasons shew.

(1.) The Cause or Means by which alone it is conveyed, if it bestow or convey only a limited Power, then it is limited in the very being of it, for there can be no more than is conveyed: Now we know, the People by their publick Act of Consent and Compact, may either bind themselves to a full subjection to the Monarchs Will guided by his own Reason; or by some constituted Rule or Law set him to govern by; which latter if they do, then is his Authority radically limited; for they owning no more subjection, he can have no farther Power.

(2.) If Soveraignty may be so limited that Active Obedience is not due to the Commands which exceed those Limits, but may lawfully be denyed to them, then it may be limited in the Power it self; For in such case the Power exceeds not the Limitation, for if the exceeding Acts were *Potestative*, we owe active subjection to them, in as much as they are the Ordinance of God to which in all things not prohibited, active Subjection is due.

(3.) If Power in the Supream be such that it can not be limited, then either because it is *God's Ordinance*; or else because it is Supream, But its being God's Ordinance hinders not; for we see, *Rom.* 13. all Powers as well Supream as Subordinate, are God's Ordinance; yet Subordinate Powers may be limited, not only in the *Rule of Acting*, but in the *Kind of Acts*; as none can deny. Neither its being *Supream*, doth hinder its *limitableness*; indeed as before, it hinders it from being capable of Confinement, in the *kind of Acts*, but *in the Measure or Rule or working*, it doth not hinder, in as much as a Soveraign Power may as well attain its end; by being confined to another Law from without, as by the Law of its own Reason, if not much better: Also we no where find God's Word making any difference, or giving Power to confine Subordinate Powers; but forbidding it of Soveraigns.

(4.) That is to be granted, which denyed, makes all Soveraigns Arbitrary, and of equal Power; but to affirm that Power is one unlimited, and investing all the Acts of the Soveraigns Will, doth so, for there is Soveraignity Arbitrary, not when it hath no *moral* bounds, for then none were or could be Arbitrary; but when Power is so fully in one that every Act of his *Arbitrium* or Will is *Potestative* and Soveraign.

(5.) I have the Judgment of all the Reformed Churches and Divines in *Germany, France, Belgia, Scotland,* on my part, who have both allowed and actually used forcible Resistance against subversive Instruments of their Soveraigns Will; yea our own Famous Princes. *Eli-*

zabeth, *James*, and *Charles* 1*ſt*. both by Edicts and Aſſiſtance have juſtified the ſame: Which they would not have done, had they bin perſwaded of ſuch an unlimited Ordinance of God in veſting all the Acts of the Will of him who is Supream. So that by all this it appears that ſome Perſons that conceit of ſuch an unlimited Ordinance of God, is a meer chimera and groundleſs conceit.

Object. Now the only Difficulty which I can think on, is this, God's Ordinance in Sovereignty, as before, is not only power to ſuch an end but ſufficiency of Power to the aſſecution of that end: Now a limited Power ſeemeth not to be ſufficient for the end of Government, becauſe there are two Powers neceſſary to the end of Government, ſc. Power of *making* and Authentick *interpreting* of Laws, which are not conſiſtant with the limitation of Power.

Anſw. It is true of Limitation in reſpect of Acts; and therefore I aver, that ſuch a Limitation cannot be where a Power is Supream. But for Limitation to a *Rule* and defined way of working I cannot ſee how it withſtands the end of Government: So that ſuppoſing Power of *making* and *interpreting* Laws be neceſſary to the end of Government, yet that they be abſolutely reſident in him who is Supream, ſc. to make Laws and interpret Laws Authoritatively without being bound to follow any Light or Rule therein, but his own Reaſon is not neceſſary to the end of Government: In theſe Acts a Regulated Power is enough in the *moſt Simple State*, ſc. a Power to *make* new Laws, if any be needful; and *interpreting* the old. if ambiguous, according to the Rule of the former eſtabliſhed Laws; and by the Advice of his Learned Council and Judges of his Supream Courts of Juſtice. We ſee in matters Spiritual, there is no Legiſlative Power reſident, to ordain or give Authentick Senſe in matters *de fide*, yet the Church ſtands well enough; one ſtanding Rule of Scripture being ſufficient with a *Miniſterial Interpretation*: So it is probable a State might, by a compleat ſtanding Rule of Law, and a Miniſterial Power of Interpretation, were there no Legiſlative Power reſident in any Supream Magiſtrate thereof.

Aſſert. 2. But the matter is far more clear in a *mixed Government*; ſo that were it neceſſary in a *Simple Government*, that the Supream ſhould be unlimited in his Power, yet in a mixed (which is enough for us in this Kingdom) evidently it is not ſo: And to make this appear, I will lay down three grounds.

(1.) Such a Government may be eſtabliſhed that the Supream Power may be placed in many Perſons, either of the ſame, or divers Condition, that is, in a mixed Subject; elſe all Forms were unlawful, except Simple Monarchy.

(2.) If this Supream Power be inequally placed in the Persons or States of Men; so that a real Sublimity and Principality be given to one, then the Denomination may be taken from that Principal: And so it is a *Monarchy*, or Aristocracy, or Democracy *mixed* in the *Power it self*.

(3.) Where the Supremacy of Power is thus in many; although all taken together, have an unlimited Power, as in ours, yet neither of them several by himself hath, or can have; for it is a contradiction, that it be resident in *many*, and yet unlimitedly in one.

Now to those two shews of Argument, which in the beginning I mentioned to the contrary I say. Before *Government* be established, it is true the People have no *Formal Politick Power* of Life and Death; yet they have a *Seminal*, that is, every one for himself, his Family and Posterity hath a Power of resigning up their Natural Liberty to be governed by one, or many; after this or that Form as they shall judge fittest. God ordaining that Powers should be to such an end, hath thereby legitimated and ratified any Consent or Contract which People may make of parting with their Liberty, and giving *Magistrates* a Common Power over them to that end. And God's not prescribing any *Rule* or *Measure* of Power by his Ordinance of Authority, hath left it in the Peoples Liberty, to resign up themselves according to such Rule and Terms, as they judge fittest, so it be such as the end of his Ordinance may be attained thereby. Thus although by it self, and excluding God's Ordinance, they have no immediate Power to lay a Command on others, nor Power of Life and Death, yet in vertue of God's Ordinance their common Consent and Contract is sufficient to set up such a Power which is endowed with a sufficiency of Command for *Government* and the *end of Government* over those which have, each Man for himself and his, set it up. So although *second Causes* have no Power by themselves to produce their Effects; yet working in vertue of the *first Cause* they have Power to produce Effects, sometimes far beyond their own measure. Therefore I desire our Opposites, either to bring some Ordinance of God expresly forbidding to set any *Bounds* or *Rule* of Power upon the *Will* of the Magistrate; or else let them suffer Mankind to use their Right in resigning up that Liberty which God and Nature hath given them upon such Terms and Conditions as they apprehend best for their own good, and the due end of Government. In the close of this Question I will lay down three Conclusions concerning the *Ordinance of God*, and the Nature of Soveraignty.

(1.) God hath ordained that in Societies of Men there should be a *Politick Power for a peaceable and Godly Life*. This Ordinance hath put a *Seminal Power* in all the Societies of Men, &c. A Liberty and Power by common Confent to refign up themfelves and theirs to one Supream; thereby conftituting a *Common Politiek Power*.

(2.) *God in his Ordinance for Government having not determined any kind of Form or Power; hath left it to the liberty of Societies of Men to choofe to which kind they will refign up themfelves*, either to a Supream Regulated in the Acts of his Will by his own Reafon, as in Abfolute Government, or to one Regulated by a *Common Reafon* or Law conftituted by publick confent, as in limited.

(3.) *God in his Ordinance for Government having not determined the Subject of this Power, hath left it to the choice of Societies to inveft with this Sovereignty, either one Perfon or many, and thofe either of the fame, or divers forts and ranks of Men*; whence arife Simple or mixed Governments, and this is the *Architectonical Power* left in Societies before they are engaged in a Government. Here is the fumm of what I aver concerning God's Ordinance in Soveraignty, which I challenge any to gainfay.

Sect. 2. Concerning the *Nature and Quality of Limitation*.

(1.) We muft confider a diftinction of Powers, which is either

1. A Simple Power of willing or doing, which is in every moral Agent.

2. A Power of Authoritative and Obligatory willing or doing, fo that an Act of it, whether a Will of Command or Cenfure expreft, hath in it a binding Power to Subjection. This is that which we call Magiftracy, of whofe Limitation now we treat.

(2.) Concerning Limitation: We muft know that it indureth an Abfolute *neceffity* of not producing any Act beyond thofe Limits. For a Power having bounds beyond which it can exceed, if it pleafe, though with difficulty it is not properly limited, but hindred.

(3.) This *neceffity* of not exceeding thofe bounds is fuch as the *bounds* themfelves are; fo that it is ever true, that a Power in what way it is limited cannot exceed thofe Limits.

(4.) There are of this Power but two forts of Limits, *fc.* (.1.) *Moral*. (.2.) *Civil*, or Politick; of which two we muft diftinctly confider.

(1.) *Moral Limits* is the Moral Will or *Law of God*; and a Power is faid to be limited by this, not when it cannot produce any Act at all; but when it cannot *morally* produce it, that is, *without fin*; for the fuperveining of a Moral bound doth not take away the *Power of doing*, but of Right or Sinlefs doing: *v.g.* in *Natural Powers*. God's prohibition of eating Swines Flefh, did not take away from the *Jew*, the Natural Power of eating it, but the Power of Sinlefs eating it: So in *Civil Power*, a prohibition of God coming upon it, doth not take away the Power of *Civil* and Authoritative doing; but of Lawful, or Sinlefs doing: And hence it follows, (1.) That moral Limitation is only of the *Exercife* of Power; not of the *Power* it felf, for the Power is not thereby taken away, but remains equally extenfe and able to all its Acts, as it was before; only now it cannot put forth it felf unto certain Acts without fin, which it could before: Thus an *Abfolute* Monarch, who hath a Power of doing, as extenfe as his reafonable Will, promifeth to do but this, or in this manner: Now he is *morally* bound by vertue of this promife, and cannot without Sin do otherwife: Yet if he do, his Commanding Power is the fame, and its Act binding to the Subject. And fo it is proportionably in Legal Governments: *Cyprian* Bifhop of *Carthage* hath by the Cannons a Power of judging Ecclefiaftical Caufes committed to him. He refolves and promifes to do nothing of moment herein, but by the confent of his Clergy, now he is morally bound, and if afterwards he do a thing by himfelf without their confent, he fins: Yet no man will fay his Epifcopal Power is leffened, or the Act he fo doth is Canonically invalid, and not obligatory.

(2.) Yea it follows alfo, that it is not properly a Limitation of the *Exercife* of Power neither, for by a moral bond, the Power is not fo bound up, but that it can *exercife* it felf, and that validly too, though not without Sin, as appears before.

(3.) Alfo that is no detractation from *Abfolutenefs* of Power, nor is it fufficient to make a diftinction of it into *Abfolute* and *Limited*. For, (1.) It caufeth no real Limitation of Power, either in the Nature, or exercife of it. (2.) It is not *diftinctive*, being to be found in the moft Abfolute Power under Heaven, all being bounded by God's Law, the Law of Equity and many promifes by themfelves made.

(2.) Civil or Legal *Limits* caufeth *Civil* and Legal definement of Authority, fo that its exceeding Acts are not *Legal* and binding, that is, are *non* Authoritative: For as a Moral Bond induces a neceffity of Confinement in *effe morali*, fo a *Civil* and *Legal* Bond doth in *effe Legali & Obligatorio*. Hence follows,

(1.) It is thefe Legal and Civil Bounds which conftitute a Government in a Limited Condition, not thofe *Moral*; for this is *diftinctive*, and is never found in an Abfolute Government, for there the Soveraign by Promife or Oath binding himfelf to a ftated Courfe, doth put no Law Civil upon his Power, or the exercife of it; for though he fin in exceeding afterwards, yet his Acts are truly Legal and Authoritative.

(2.) This induceth a real Limitation of Power, neither can it be only of exercife; for fith it brings an illegality and un-authoritativenefs on Acts exceeding, that is, makes them none in *effe Civili & Politico*, it is a Limitation of Power it felf; for when a Power can produce no potential Acts beyond fuch Limits, then it is limited in the very being. (3.) *Acts*

(3.) *Acts exceeding Politick and Legal Limitation*, being not Legal nor Authoritative in that state, can give no Authority to the Instruments, and therefore they may be resisted without resistance or violation of Authority. Whereas it is otherwise in *Acts exceeding* moral *Limitation*; for being Authoritative, they authorise the Instrument, and give him an unresistance.

In summ; Limitation Moral and Civil or Legal do differ in three main particulars.

(1.) *Moral*, sith it is no Politick or Authoritative Act, makes no real detraction either in Power or Exercise of it, and therefore agrees with the most Absolute Government: whereas *Legal* being a Politick and Authoritative Act, makes a real diminution; and so is the *ratio formalis*, or *distinctive conceit* constituting Limited Government; nor can be found in Absolute.

(2.) Hence, *exceeding Acts* notwithstanding *moral* Limitation are Authoritative, proceed from Gods Ordinance and Challenge Subjection: But they are otherwise which *exceed* a Legal Limitation.

(3.) *Exceeding* Acts in *Moral* Limitation being authoritative, have the Sword or Compelling Power annexed to them, which may not be resisted; but in *Legal* being not Authoritative, they have not the Sword or Compelling Power annexed, and therefore may be resisted in their Instruments: I will illustrate all this by a familiar instance, in our Government a Judge hath a Commission to hear and determine Causes according to the Verdict of Twelve Men. Here is a Power limited in the very being, that is, Legally and Civilly. This Judge useth indirect means to corrupt the Jury to bring in an unjust Verdict; but judgeth as his Commission binds him according to their Verdict: Here is a *moral exceeding*, yet the Act of Judgment is Authoritative, because according to his Commission, and must not be resisted: Again he passeth Sentence in another Cause expresly against the Verdict of the Jury, in an Arbitrary way. Here is a Legal Exceeding, and the Sentence is not Authoritative. He having no such Power committed to him, the Sentence can have no binding Power in it.

Sect. 3. Thirdly, Concerning the *Causes* and *Means* of Limitation: Some there be who suppose

(1.) That *Radical Limitation*, that is of the Power it self, requires *an express and notorious Act*, it must be done in the beginning, and at once.

(2.) That *a Prince may so limit himself, as not to require to be actively subjected to, and yet be limited only in the Exercise, not in the Power it self.*

(3.) That *no Limitation by after condescent, is of the Power it self.* This being a consequent from the first.

Now that the Falshood of thefe and the like grounds may appear, let us a little more diligently handle the *Caufes* and *Means of Limitation*, which, as before, being two-fold, Moral and Civil; we will begin with Moral.

(1.) Now the *formal Caufe* of a meer *moral* Limitation, is that which morally bounds or makes finful any Act of Power. We are therefore to inquire what it is which can do that: And this is (1.) Principally the *Moral Law of God* forbidding fuch an Exercife of Power. This is an *univerfal, perpetual*, and *invincible* Limitation of all Powers of Government, either Abfolute or Legal, yea of all active power of reafonable Creatures.

Caufes of Moral Limitation.

(2.) There is another mean of Limitation Moral, fc. *a Promife*, *Oath, or pofitive Conflitution*, whereby a Prince puts a Bond upon himfelf, making that now finful to be done, which before was not fo. This alfo induceth a *moral* Limitation, as well in *Abfolute* as *Legal* Governments; as if an Abfolute Monarch promife to follow fuch a *Rule*, which hath a power to ufe any which his *Reafon* fhall dictate. Or if a *Legal* promife to abridge himfelf in a courfe, in which the Law hath left him indeterminate: In this refpect, they come under a *moral* Limitation: But concerning this *pofitive mean*, we muft note,

(1.) This promife how folemn foever it be, muft be a fimple Bond: It muft extend to no *diminution* of Power, or *difcharge* from Duty of fubjection; for then it is not meerly Moral, it makes the exceeding Act not only finful, but *non*-obliging: Whereas it is the note of a meer *moral Bond* that it extends not to any leffening of Authority, or difcharge of Duty: As if a Captain take his Enemy Prifoner, he to fave his Life fwears *him* a full Vaffalidge afterwards, his Mafter promifes to command him only fuch Services, never abfolving him from his former Bond of Abfolute Slavery; Here is a *moral Bond*; yet ftill a full debt of fubjection in cafe the Mafter fhould break his Word, and put him on other employment.

(2.) If the matter be more throughly lookt into this *poffitive mean* of Limitation is either none at all; or elfe adds nothing to the former, of the *Moral Law of God*: For in fuch *Promife* or *Oath* whereby a Governour limits himfelf, there is an *exprefs* or *tacite* condition, if it conduce to the end of Government, the Glory of God, and publick good: For if fuch Oath or Bond hinder the end of Government, it is *eo nomine*, unlawful and invalid; but if conduce to it, then it was no more than was vertually required of him before by the Moral Law; this *Promife* or *Oath* being but a more folemn profeffion and proteftation to do that which before implicitely he was bound morally unto. Thus we fee, if the Monarchs power in the State were only morally as the Captive Slave to his Master; and all our Laws and Statutes being but moral Limitations of this second sort, are not so much as moral Limitation any farther than the Prince sees them conduce to the end of Goment, if any seem to stand in his way, and hinder him therein, he is no longer bound to it, but may account it an ill made Promise or Oath which is better broke than kept.

(2.) Of the *Causes* and *Means* of *Civil and Legal Limitations*, whereby not only the *Exercise*, but the *Power* it self is confined. *Causes of Legal limitation.*

(1.) The *formal Causes* hereof is the limitation of the *Duty* of *Subjection* in the people: The *Duty* of subjection is the Original of the *Power* of Authority. People by becoming Debtors of subjection, do set up Authority; and by stinting and terminating the Duty of Subjection do put bounds and terms to the power of Commanding.

(2.) Let us see then by what means the Duty of Subjection may be terminated. I conceive it may be done two wayes.

1. At first when a people resigning up themselves to a state of Subjection do it not Absolutely, but impose only a Limited Bond on themselves; for if they impose no more *Duty*: The Governour can assume no more *Power*. Now this may be done not only by *possitive* Express and notorious Act; but also by a *negative*; a meer not imposing of an Absolute Bond of Duty on themselves is enough: So that if it cannot be proved either by *Records* of the first Institution, or *present Obligation* that a people have put themselves into a state of *Absolute* Subjection, then it is to be held but *Limited*: For whatsoever is ours by the *Law of Nature*, cannot be taken from us but by some *possitive Act* done by our selves or Ancestors: Thus in private Men; Liberty which is mine by Nature, none can take from me unless he can bring a Title or Right whereby it became his, and I his Servant, nor am I any farther his Servant than he can bring proof of his Right, the same is true of a Society of Men. In this case it belongs to the *Challenger*, and not to the *Defendant* to bring his *possitive notorious Act* for proof of his Title, and measure of his Title. So that the Demand of those is unreasonable, who standing for a full right in our Government, puts on the people part to bring Evidence that they have not. Rather it is just, that they should bring some possitive and notorious Act wherein it appears that this people have fully resigned up their Liberty to an Absolute Government; or make it appear that it is God's Ordinance that where ever a people do constitute a Soveraign Power, they must make an absolute Resignation of their Liberty.

2. By after Condescent, for this may be *a mean of Civil Limitation*, unless any will imagine that a people once putting themselves into Absolute

folute Subjection, are irrevocably so. And thus a Monarch becomes *limited*, when the Promise or Oath he limits himself by, is not *Simple*, but amounts either expresly or equivalently to a *Relaxation of the Bond of Subjection*: Whether it proceed from meer Grace, or Conscience of Equity, or by Petition, or Importunity of the people, it matters not what was the ground of it, if it carry with it a *Relaxation of the Duty of Subjection*, it is a *mean of Civil Limitation*, in the very *root of Power*; for *Power* can be no larger in the Prince, than *Duty* of Subjection is in the people; for these two have a necessary Dependance and Relation of Equality either to other. Thus if a Monarch, taking advantage of force of Arms, impose a new Oath of *full subjection* on his People, who before were but *legally* bound; and prevail so far that the *whole* or *major part* of his People do take it for themselves and theirs, here is a *change* of Government from *Legal* into *Absolute*, and enlargement of Power: So on the contrary. And for this matter we need look no farther than the *National Oath*, or *Established Laws*; for if they bind the People to an *Absolute Subjection*, such is the Power; and though it have *Moral*, yet it hath no Legal Limitation: And so on the contrary if they bind only to a *subjection according to the Law*; the Government is limited in the very *Power* of it. Hence it appears to be false which some say, *That a Monarch may so tye himself as to require not to be subjected to, but according to such Laws*, and yet not be civilly limited, in his very Power; for if he so far require not to be subjected to, that he untie the Bond of Subjection beyond those Laws; then is his Authority limited, and can proceed no farther? neither are the Instruments of his Will exceeding those Laws, authorized but private persons, and resistable: And also false, which others say, *That Limitation by condescent cannot be radical.*

Now if inquiry be made concerning the simplicity of Ancient Forms of assuming into Soveraignty, as when the People are said to make one King, to indue him *indefinitely* with Kingly Power, not confining his Government by any express Limitation.

Answ. I conceive in such case to know how far a People are bound by such an *indefinite Contract*, these things are to be lookt into.

(1.) If the *intent* of the People can be discovered in such a Constitution, for if it can, doubtless the Contract binds so far, and no farther. Thus *Lyra* concludes concerning the request of the People of *Israel* for a King, that it is to be understood of an Absolute King, by that clause in the Petition, 1 *Sam.* 8. 5. A King to judge us like all the Nations, for all those *Eastern* Nations having Absolute Monarchs, they desiring to be governed like them; must be conceived to intend such a Government.

(2.) If there be no Expression of their *intention* : Then a Light concerning it must be borrowed from Circumstances ; *sc.* the kind of Government whereunto they have been formerly accustomed, or that of the Nation from which they proceeded : And thus the *Saxons* giving Kingly State to their Captains in this Land, cannot in reason be interpreted to intend any other, than that whereunto they were *accustomed*, and which was the *form* of the Nation whence they came. This Rule is ever to be kept as well in publick as in private Contracts of that simple indefinite Form, that *they are to be construed, as far as may be in favour of the Granter*.

CHAP. II.

Concerning the Constitution of this Monarchy, its Original: The Limitation and Mixture of it vindicated.

COncerning the *Saxons* Entrance, I said it was not a Conquest, *sc.* properly and simply, but an Expulsion : To which is answered, this is not true, nor greatly material. I reply, it is both *true* and *material*, it is *true* ; for all the *Britains* which retained their Name and Nation were they many or few, were expelled into *Wales* : All the rest *in gentem, leges, nomen, linquamq* ; *vincentium concesserunt*; as saith Mr. *Cambden*. And it is very material, for if they which only remained here *in gentem & leges vincentium concesserunt* : Then the Conquerers kept their *old form of Government* : The *Saxons* came not into the condition of the Conquered *Britains*, but they into the old Liberty of the *Saxons*. Hereupon grew there a necessity of inquiry into the Government of the Nation, before they came hither ; that so we might know what a one they established here, and brought the remaining *Britains* into ; and a Record of more unquestionable Authority than *Tacitus* I could not imagine : Nor a more express Testimony for a limited form in the very *potestas* of it ; of which sort he affirms the Government of all the *Germain* Nations was,

(1.) That they were a People of *Germany* before they came in hither is greatly probable ; for the *Angli* which accompanied them in that Invasion, were questionless *Germains*, and reckoned by *Tacitus* among that People ; doubtless they were Neighbours in Habitation which were joyned in that Voyage and Conquest.

(2.) Suppose the matter were not clear of the *Saxons*, yet is it of the *Angli* which gave denomination to the Land and People, who no doubt

doubt retained their Laws and Government says *Cambden*; which was limited in the very *Royal Power* saith *Tacitus*. I endeavour not to deduce the very *Model* of our present Government from that *Saxon* ingress: But all I aim at, is to make it appear that in *semine*, in the rude beginnings it is so ancient, and shall affirm the limited Power of the *English* Kings, and Liberty of the Subjects: To have been from thence continued till now. The *Saxons* gave no Tenure by Conquest to their Princes, but kept their Laws, and came not under the Title of a Conquered People.

Concerning the *Norman* Entrance, to prove that *William* held this Land by Conquest; some cite Mr. *Cambden* that in *Victoriæ quasi Tropheum, he disposed of the Lands of the Conquered, changed their Tenure, abrogated what English Laws and Customs he pleased*, &c. Indeed when he had gotten full possession, he did what he pleased, but *factum non probat jus*. That of Mr. *Cambden*, that the Kings of this Land have *potestatem Supremam & merum Imperium*, is no more than that of the *Statute* some speak of, that it is an Empire governed by one Supream Head, which we acknowledge; for hatt *merum Imperium* must be understood in a moderate sense, else it proves more than our Antagonists profess to own: Though Mr. *Cambden's* Judgment in this case is not of the Authority of a proof. If History and Antiquity be required as Evidence in this case, he who doth affirm such a Title of Power in our Kings, ought to shew how, and when it was conveyed to them, because he which challengeth a Right to that which was once undoubtedly mine, must prove his Right, and he can have no more than he can bring Evidence for. But if I must prove mine, there are but two wayes to prove my *Negative*, one is by *Records of History*, setting out the *first Constitution* of a State, and the Terms on which the People resigned up their Liberty to a Subjection. So in the Ancient *Roman* State, the *Venetian*, the late *Belgick Union*, and others, which have at once, visibly and lately been composed, it is likely that way might be taken. The other is by *Demonstrative Collections* drawn from the institution of the present Composure of a State. Thus alone is it possible to discern and prove the *Constitution* of a Government which springs not up at once, but by unseen degrees and moments, whose Fundamental Constitutive Acts stand upon no Record. This is the Condition of most Governments in the World which have sprung from small rude and unknown beginnings. And of this in particular. For, 1. A Limitation of Royal Power was brought hither by the *Saxons* and *Angli* our Ancestors, hath been proved. This was, as those times were, very *rude* and unpolished, it is likely such as Captains in Armies have, who can do nothing of moment without the advice and consent of the *Council of War*.

2. This

2. This Limitation of Power and Liberty received some more *formal* and setled bounds afterwards by *Customs* and Laws before the Conquest, as appears by the *common* Laws, which are as it were the *basis* and *foundation* of this Government, the Statute Laws being but after Superstructives: These Common Laws did not grow up at once, but by degrees, and were unwritten *Customs* and *Usages* gaining Authority by unknown prescription, above all written Laws; and were afterwards committed to Writing by Men skilful in the Laws.

3. At length and after the Conquest it was perfected to this *Parliamentary form*; and even this being at first but *rude* grew to this *exactness* by length of time, and infinite Contentions. This latter way only being left us; the Author takes, and no Man hath cause to despise it. For when a thing of present state is made evident by reason drawn from palpable Experience of its present Composure, it is madness to deny it to be so, because I cannot tell when it began to be so: Yea, when the question is of *present State*, it is a surer way to find out the Truth, than by Records of its Original Constitution: For in time the frame of a State may receive real variations from what it was at first, as the *Roman* State, and most others have done; for the Contracts of Men are at pleasure alterable; and an Argument drawn from Monuments of first Coalition, would then be fallacious. To the Authors First, Third, Fourth, and Fifth Arguments, proving Limitation, *page* 31, one answereth, that they prove only Limitation in the exercise of Power, Why so? *Neither the denomination of Liege nor any prescription can make us believe, that the limitations of Power had any other beginning than voluntary condescent.* As if a Government by voluntary condescent might not receive a radical Limitation. But it lies on him to prove, it was by such condescent; if he can bring no Record for it, it must in Justice be held Original, and *ab initio*. Those two denominations of *Liege Soveraign*, and *Liege People* do prove the very *Soveraignty and Subjection Legal*; but that is not so, which hath only a moral Limitation, the Denominations argue the *Bond 'twixt them to be legal*: And when Subjects have such a Liberty by Custom and Law, that they owe no farther Subjection, then (when or however they come by it) yet the very Power of the Monarch is limited, unless any will put a vain Power in the Prince, to which no Subjection is due. It is misspent time in considering only what this Government was in its *Original*; as if it must needs remain still such as it was at first; and could not receive any alterations, and gradual accomplishments in process of time. And to affirm our King hath Right by Conquest, is to say he may use an Arbitrary Power if he will: And if he hath a right of Arbitrariness, it is his lenity he doth not use it. Whoever will have a Government

vernment Abſolute, muſt prove it, if he will have it ſo. To the Reaſons for mixture in Treatiſe, *pag.* 40. which are three, there may be anſwered to the firſt of them, It is not neceſſary the mixture ſhould be in the Power: But it is ſufficient if there be a concurrence of Perſons, whoſe conſent is required to the Exerciſe of Power.

This is anſwer to the Concluſion, but nothing to the Antecedent.

(1.) And indeed if it be mixt of theſe three, the Anſwer is againſt *common ſenſe,* that a *mixture of Monarchy, Ariſtocracy* and *Democracy* ſhould be ſatisfied by annexion of Perſons to the Monarch, having meer conſent: for theſe are *Names of Power, of Government;* for *Ariſtocracy* and *Democracy* are *Powers* not *Perſons,* as well as Monarchy; therefore a Compoſition of theſe three muſt be all of *Powers.*

(2.) And indeed this *Chimera* of a *mixture* in the *exerciſe of Power,* is plain Nonſenſe: For a mixture in the Acts or exerciſe ſuppoſeth a mixture in the *Principles of Action,* that is, in the very Powers: A *mixt Act* proceeding from a *Simple Power* is ſuch ſtuff that I never heard before. Now if a *mixture in Acts* argues a *mixture in Powers,* theſe *Powers* muſt be *Co-ordinate* and Supream: For *Subordinates* make no mixture: Alſo Powers concurrent to Supream Acts, ſuch as *Legiſlation* is confeſt to be, cannot be but Supream Powers, neither can any Man living clear from *pure Nonſenſe, ſc.* This *Co-ordination is but to ſome Act or Exerciſe of the Supream Power, not in the Power it ſelf:* For *concourſe* to an Act, implyes a *Power of concurrence,* and *concourſe to a Supream Act,* argues a *Supream Power;* for an inferiour Power cannot afford a Co-ordinate concurrence to a Supream Act. But here it may be ſaid,

" If the mixture be in the Supremacy of Power, how can the King
" be the only Supream and Head. Unleſs he be the Crown or top of
" the Head, for they alſo muſt be our Head and our Soveraigns, if
" they be mixt in the Supremacy of Power. To which I here Anſwer,

1. That the Titles of *Head* and *Supream* are fully ſatisfied by this, that he is the ſole Principle and Fountain from whence the Execution of all Law and Juſtice flows to his People by inferiour Officers and Courts, all whoſe Authority is derivatively from him as its Head.

(2.) That theſe Titles in proper Conſtruction import only *utmoſt Chiefty,* nor do they agree to any kind of Right in the Fundamental and Radical Powers of a Kingdom; but to the Principal and Tranſcendant Intereſt: Another may have a Right in the Supream Power, yet not be *Supream,* nor *Head;* becauſe not having a Supremacy in that Power: So it is in the *Colledges,* the Fellows have a Fundamental Intereſt in the Power of Government, yet that hinders not, but that the Title of *Head* and *Chief* is given to him who is Governour. Alſo in the *Natural Body,* from whence the *Metaphor* of *Head* is borrowed, are three

Fundamental and Radical Powers fcituate in the three principal parts: yet none will fay, the *Heart* and *Liver* are *Heads* too, becaufe they partake of the *Supream Powers* of Nature: Is not the *Legiflative* Power the *Supream*? Have not the *Houfes* an *Authoritative Concurrence* and influx into that bufinefs.

To the fecond Argument for Radical mixture, which is from the *Legiflative* Power being in all three may be anfwered, *That phrafe is fatisfied and explained by that concurrence and confent in the Exercife of Supream Power:* To which I reply, is a *Legiflative Power* fati fied by a bare *powerlefs confent*: I demand, is that *confent Caufal and Authoritative*; or meerly *Conciliary* and *Unauthoritative*? And whereas they have an enacting Authority by that received and fet claufe in the beginning of Acts: *Be it enacted by the King's moft Excellent Majefly, and the Authority of the Lords and Commons affembled in Parliament.* I ask, whether that claufe, which as exprefly as Words can, afcribes an enacting Authority to them, be fatisfied by fuch a Power of afienting? But they tell us of a former Phrafe which ran thus: *The King by the Advice and Confent of the Prelates, Earls, and Barons, and at the Inftance and Requeft of the Commonalty hath ordained*, &c. Suppofe anciently fome Statutes run under that form; that *advife* and *Inftance* muft be underftood of an *Authoritative* and *enacting Advice* and *Inftance*, as the latter forms explain it: For it is equal that the latter expound the former, and not the contrary; for fuch *a Power of Confenting* (if it be neceffary) is indeed a *Power of Enacting*; for though in *tranfient Acts* one may ftand by and confent to the doing, and yet not be *efficient*, yet in *immanent Acts* which are done, *per immediatum Volitionem*, by a meer expreffion of the Will, a *concurrence in Confenting*, and a *concurrence in Doing* is one and the same thing: Now *Legiflation* is an *immanent Act*, confifting in a meer *expreffion of an Authoritative Will*.

To the Third Argument which is from *the end of mixture to moderate and reftrain*, &c. may be Anfwered,

" If the Fundamental Conftitution had intended them fuch a Power,
" it would not have left a Power in the Monarch to call, or diffolve
" them, which would make this Power of theirs altogether ineffectual.

This Reafon. (1.) Whatever ftrength it hath had in it, now it hath none; becaufe that Power of Diffolving is now by Law fufpended, for this Parliament; and after it is a neceffity by Law imperfect of reducing that Power of calling Parliaments into Act every Three Years.

(2.) Neither was it true before thefe Acts, that fuch a Power was left in the Monarch at pleafure to ufe or not; for it was by Ancient Laws determined how often they fhould be Convocated.

(3.) But being granted that this Power is simply and fully in the Monarch, yet I deny, that hence it follows, that it would *make that Power of the Houses altogether ineffectual*; because that *de facto*, though it hath been in the Monarch so long, yet it never hath made it void; but they have exercised a limiting Power, as Histories relate enough, yea, and sometimes too much, over the Monarch, notwithstanding his Power of Calling and Dissolving them. Thus in the *Colledges*, the *Fellows* have an effectual, and more than moral limiting Power, though the *Governour* hath the Power of *Calling* and *Dissolving* their Meetings. And Anciently the prime *Patriarch* had the Power of *Calling* and *Dissolving General Counsels*, yet they had a *Power of Limiting*, yea of *Censuring* him for Exorbitances for all that. The Reason is, because many things fall out of in a Government, inducing such Necessities on the Monarch, that he for their supply will choose to reduce such Power into Act of Calling, and suspend such Power of dissolving, although he know those States will use their limiting Power in reducing such Exorbitancies, and punishing those dearest Instruments which have been used in them. This the *Constitutors* of this frame preconsidering might put in the Monarch this Power, and yet intend to the other States a *Legal* and *Effectual* power of restraining his Exorbitances, by using Force not against him, but its procures and Instruments. Thus we see, there is no need of entring on that Dispute, whither this Power of Calling and Dissolving the Houses be placed in the Monarch; as all his other are, not Absolutely, but with limitation of necessary reducing it into Act, on the last Exigencies of the Kingdom.

If the Monarch's Power in *England* be unlimited, I query,

(1.) Why in the Oath proposed to be taken by all his Majesties Subjects the Power of *enacting Statutes* is sworn to be jointly in the *King's Majesty, Lords* and *Commons in Parliament*.

Oath printed at Oxon.

(2.) Why we are enjoyned to swear that *we do believe the Subjects* of England *are not obliged by any Act made either by the King's Majesty solely, or the Houses solely*, &c. If Power be solely his, then an Act made by him solely is obliging. If they be not *Obligatory*, they are not *Authoritative*, and so the mixture and limitation is in the Authority it self. Here is no place left for the distinction of *Active* and *Passive Subjection*. For,

(1.) Will any think that the intent is to swear Men to be bound not to do, but to suffer?

(2.) The *belief of a non-Obligation* proceeds indifferently, and as fully concerning the *sole Acts* of the *King*, as the *Houses*.

(3.) I would know if the *States* do limit only *morally*, what do they, which is not done without them? A *Promise* and *Oath* do limit morally without them. You will say they may admonish him, and deny their consent, and so make his Acts invalid: you mean still *morally invalid*; and so would they be without them.

(4.) Suppose the Monarch minded to establish a Law, which he judges needful, and the States being averse, he *enacts* it without them? Is it not a Law? It hath all the Legislative Authority in it. You will say it is not duly made.

(1.) I grant it: But yet it is a *Law*, for it hath all the Power of a Law.

(2.) But it is not duly made, Why *the Power of last decision* is in the *King alone*: Suppose he define that the *intent* of his Predecessors in granting this *consenting Power* to the *Houses* had no intent to hinder, but further themselves in establishing good Laws; and therefore now they not concurring by assent to this needful Act, he ought not to be hindred, but may lawfully do it without them. He is the *last Judge* in this *case*; and it must be held ever *lawfully enacted*. So that in the result here is left to these *States* by these grounds neither *Civil* nor *Moral Limitation*, but at pleasure.

(5.) If Limitation in our Government exempts Subjects from a necessity of *Active* Subjection; but not from *Passive*: How is it that our Laws do not only determine what the Monarch shall *Command*, but also what he shall inflict: What shall be accounted Rebellion, what Felony, &c. And what not; also what he shall inflict for this and that Crime, and what not? Sith the Law limiting what he shall *Command*, do limit our necessity of *Active Subjection*; it will follow, that the Laws limiting what he shall inflict, do limit our necessity of *Passive Subjection*. Here is no evasion by saying the Laws do limit him morally what he shall inflict, and if he inflict beyond Law, he sins in it; but we must suffer: For our Antagonists acknowledge that the Laws defining what he shall *command* do so limit our Active Subjection, that we have a *simple exemption* from any necessity of *doing*; and therefore also the Laws defining what he shall inflict, doth so limit our passive Subjection, that we have a *simple exemption* from any necessity of suffering, beyond those limitations; for also, if they did not free us from Passive Subjection, it were unlawful not only to *resist*, but also to *avoid* suffering even by flight.

(6.) When the Liberties of *Magna Charta*, and others Grants have been gotten and preserved, and recovered at the rate of so much Trouble, Suit, Expence and Blood, whither by all that ado was intended only a Moral Liberty, definement in the Monarch, and not also of the Power it self; only that he might not lawfully exorbitate from established Laws, and not also that he might have no Authority or Power to exorbitate at all? Sure this was their aim, for the former he could not do before.

(7.) The Law granting a *Writ* of *Rebellion* against him who refuseth to obey the Sentence of the Judge, though he have an express Act of the King's Will to warrant him: Doth it not suppose those *exceeding and extrajudicial Acts of the King's Will* to be unauthoritative, and unable to priviledge a Man from resistance? It is very remarkable, that the late King *Charles* in all his *Declarations* which I have seen, doth not once touch upon this way, &c. a Challenge of such a Latitude of Authority as can preserve destructive Instruments from force; but condemns the now Resistance by solemn *Protestations* of Innocency, and intentions of governing by the known Laws.

CHAP. III.

Of Resistance in Relation to several kinds of Monarchy.

TWO things our Opponents propose, in relation to several kinds of Monarchy, unto us:

(1.) To consider how we *state the point of Resistance in the kinds of Government*.

I refer not this case to the Consciences of Men as to an *Authoritative Judge*, but a *moral principle of discerning Right*: and who can deny unto Man such a Liberty to conceive of Right according to the Light he hath from the Fundamentals of a State?

Let the Judicious read what is said hereabout in Treatise *Cap. 6. Sect. 2.* and tell me how the Question can be otherwise determined, unless you overthrow *Monarchy*, by giving a final Judgment to the *States*; or all *Liberty*, if you give it to the Monarch, and supposing the *aim at subversion* be evident to Mens Consciences, can we deny them a Natural Power of judging according to that Evidence; or Liberty of assisting the Wronged?

Appeal must be to the Community (in my Treatise I say) *as if there were no Government.* To which may be replyed, " This Appeal is disadvanta-
" gious to the Monarch; for they will be more ready to believe their
" Representative: This would in the consequence be dangerous, the high way to Confusion.

Answ. 1. I say, not *simply* that People are at liberty, as if there were no Government; but in this *particular Question*, bound still as before, in all besides.

Answ. 2. By

Answ. 2. By *Community* is not to be understood the *Commons* only, but *Genus humanum* especially of that Kingdom.

Answ. 3. The *Reason of Mankind* will not be partial towards their *Representatives*, for in so great a question *Wise Men* cannot be blinded: *Honest Men* will go according to their Conscience, and *Reasonable Men* according to Evidence, and will see it concerns them as well to avoid *Anarchy* by aiding a wronged *Monarch*, as *Tyranny*, by aiding an Opprest *State*.

But sith I find many bitter Enveighers against an *Appeal* to the *Conscience of Mankind*, in this last case so uncapable of an Authoritative Decision:

(1.) Let them consider on what Foundation God hath built Monarchy and all other Powers, but on the Consciences of Men, *Rom.* 13.

(2.) Let them weigh whither, when they say all they can say, such an Appeal be avoidable: For,

1. If a Controversie arise between the *King* and a particular Person or Place; the King shall judge it in his Courts by his Judges, and the Sentence shall be executed by the Force and Arms of his other Subjects.

2. If it be between *Him* and the *Representatives* of his whole Kingdom, and Supream Court of Judicature in which the Acts and Persons of all other Courts and Judges are to be judged. The King cannot judge this in his other Courts and by his Judges; nor yet by himself; for a King out of his Courts cannot judge in a Legal Goyernment, especially the Acts of his Supream Court. But be it so: Suppose an Agreement in this, that the King by himself is the ultime Judge of Controversies: Yet it is very like these *States* with whom the contention is, will not yield him so, to judge against them, in his own cause. But suppose they do not submit to his Determination: He will say then they sin, and rebel against him. Well, let it be granted, yet submit they do not: I demand in this case, what Course the King hath to make effectual his Sentence? It must be by force of Arms, by the Sword: But of whom? Either the Peoples whose Representatives they are, or other Mens: But what shall bind them to afford their Force to make good his Sentence? it must be their Conscience of his Right: Thus when all is done and said, to the *Consciences* of *Men* must his *Appeal* be; and to them must he make evident his Right, in this Extream Contention. Yea Doctor *Fern* in a Controversie of the like Nature, is compelled to acknowledge as much: For the Pleaders put the case, If a King be distracted, I may add, If his Title be dubious, *&c.* The Doctors Answer is, *If it be clear that a King is so,* &c. But who shall determine this if? Must not self-Evidence in the Consciences of Men? This is all the Judicial Power the Doctor can refer us to in these cases.

Lastly,

Laſtly, Would you know what Power there is in a Community to make reſiſtance, ſome will ſay a *Parliamentary and Legal*, not *Military and Forcible*, thus they ſpeak of theſe as Contradiſtinct, when they are Subordinate, *Forcible* being ſubſervient to *Legal* to make it valid and effectual, which elſe were merely moral and ineffectual. But that is very ſtrange which ſome affirm, namely, *That if they uſe a Legal reſtraining Power, the Monarch cannot alter the Eſtabliſhed Frame*. *Sure, by cannot* they underſtand ſaliciouſly, a *moral* cannot, that is; not without Sin; which is a poor ſmall *cannot* now-a-days: If they mean indeed *cannot*, that is, is not *able*, it is againſt Reaſon by their grounds; for what is not he able to do, whoſe loweſt, moſt deſperate Inſtrument of Pleaſure is unreſiſtable, let them remember where it is ſaid, *A Forcible Conſent cannot be wanting to a Conquerrer*; and a Conquerours Power is no more than unreſiſtable; nay I am ſenſleſs on their grounds, if he cannot *lawfully*: For ſuppoſe he be pleaſed to make it a queſtion, Whither he were not better govern by the *Civil Law*, as more conducent to God's Glory, and the end of Government? He is by Law the laſt Judge of this queſtion, if he determine it beſt; then we may lawfully do it.

Sect. 2. They propoſe unto us to prove, *That limitation and mixture in Monarchy do not imply a forcible conſtraining Power in Subjects, for the preventing of Diſſolution, but only a legal.*

Anſw. They fail in the very propoſal of their Aſſertion in three points!

(1.) They propoſe it of Limitation in general; whereas I grant it of that which is *only in Exerciſe*; affirming it only of that which is of the Power it ſelf.

(2.) They ſay *forcible conſtraining Power in Subjects*, when they ſhould have ſpecified againſt *Subverſive Inſtruments*, for I grant it of the Monarch himſelf.

(3.) They oppoſe *Forcible* to *Legal*, when it ſhould be oppoſed only to *meer Moral*, not to Legal as before.

Their Arguments are,

1. *Such a Power muſt be in them by reſervation, and then it muſt be expreſt in the Conſtitution of the Government and Covenant, or elſe by implication.*

Anſw. 1. There is a *Reſervation of Liberty*, or Power of not being ſubject neither Actively nor Paſſively to the exceeding Acts of the Monarchs Will: This is by *Implication*, for what they did not reſign up, they did reſerve.

(2.) A Power of Authoritative judging and reſiſting the Monarch thus exceeding: This neither expreſly nor implicitely is reſerved; not becauſe

because it is *unlawful*, but contradictory to the very Institution of a Monarchy, and so, under that intention, *Impossible*.

(3.) *A Power of forcible resistance* of subversive Instruments: This by the Authority of the Law, is, not *reserved*, but expresly committed, not only, to the Houses of Parliament, but all inferiour Courts; for the Law, whose Execution the King committeth to them, commands them not only to resist, but punish its Violaters, much more its Subvertors, without exception of *Persons* or respect of their *Number*, or *Ground* and Reason why they do it, whether with or against the King's private and absolute Will or Warrant, supposing such Men to be without Warrant: And this Power of judging all Violaters and Subverters of Laws being committed to them, includes a Power of imploying the force of Arms of the County or Kingdom; if need be to make good the Sentence of the Law against them: This *Power* being a necessary attendant to the former. And they who have the *Power of judging* by Commission, have the *Power of Force* by implication. Against this reserve *by implication* they argue,

1. *Limitation cannot infer it*, &c.

Answ. Limitation in Exercise only doth not, but in the Power it self doth infer it; as the Treatise sheweth.

2. *The inconveniences of Exorbitances cannot infer ti.* *Answ.* They do not infer it of themselves, for they are the same in Absolute Rule: But supposing a People minding their frame effectually to prevent those inconveniencies, that doth infer it.

3. *The consent and intention of the People, choosing a Monarch cannot infer it; because it is not the measure of the Power it self.*

Answ. The Treatise herein before proves it.

4. *The intention of the People in procuring Limitation of Power cannot infer it.*

Answ. If the Peoples intention in it, be a greater security from Oppression than in an Absolute Government they can have, or a meer Moral Limitation can give them, then it doth infer it.

5. *If the Achitects did intend such a forcible Power to these States, they would not have left it in his Power to dissolve them.*

Answer'd fully before.

CHAP. IV.

Of places of Scripture out of the Old Testament.

ALthough enough hath been already said, yet because Doctor *Fern* saith the Monarchies of Old were of such institution as excluded Resistance. And the Prophets never called it. I will here Answer,

I grant it doth exclude it, as far as in an *Absolute Monarchy* it may be excluded; and therefore there is no need of answering his Arguments. But yet let us consider them sith he is so large in them. To shew us the *institution* of that Kingdom he brings, 1 *Sam.* 8. 11. where he says we have it; for *Samuel* is commanded, *verse* 9. to tell the People (*Jus Regis*:) Now this *Jus Regis* he makes a great matter of, and tells us, *It implies not a right of doing such unjust Acts, but a security from resistance and force, if he doth them.*

Answ. 1. It is no prejudice to the Cause I defend, if I should grant all he would work out of this Text; for it proves no farther than of that particular Kingdom, inducing no necessity that all others must have the same Institution. Also that which he concludes is but a security for the Person of the Prince from force if he do such unjust Acts; which we grant him not only in that, but all Monarchies, even the most limited.

(2.) If he have any farther reach, and would conclude out of it a *general binding Ordinance* of security from Resistance; extending even to subversive Instruments of Will. The World will wonder at him for such an audacious conclusion from such premises. All is grounded on his Interpretation of *Jus Regis*.

The Original Words in this place are not to be translated *Jus Regis*, the *Right of the King*: Because,

1. There is another more fit signification of them: The Words are משפטו now the word משפט being applied to unjust Acts, as here it is, ought not to be rendred *jus* but *mos*, not *Right*, but *manner*, as appears by another place answerable to this, 1 *Sam.* 27. 11. וזה משפטו speaking of *David's* roving, *This would be his manner*: It were be ridiculous to render it this would be his *Right* or *Priviledge*.

2. That rendring of it, cannot be justified by any other Text of Scripture; for wheresoever it is rendred *Jus*, it imports a Moral Right, not a priviledge or security in ill doing. Neither doth *Calvin* mean such a *jus* as is an *Absolute immunity* or security from Resistance: But only from

Chap. IV.   *Treatise of Monarchy.*   89

from *private men*; not of the *States of a Kingdom*, in their publick Meetings: for he expresly teacheth the same truth, *Instit. lib.* 4. *cap.* 20. and in the 31 *Numb.* which here and in the Treatise is asserted. Hear him speaking his judgment, *De privatis hominibus semper loquor : Nam si qui nunc sunt populares magistratus ad moderandam Regum libidinem consliuti (quales olim erant, qui Lacedemoniis regibus oppositi erant, Ephori ; aut Romanis Consulibus, Tribuni plebis; aut Atheniensium Senatui, Demarchi ; & qua etiam forte potestate (ut nunc res habent) funguntur in singulis regnis tres ordines, cum primarios conventus peragunt) adeo illos senocienti Regum licentie pro officio intercedere non veto, ut si Regibus impotenter grassantibus, & humili plebecula insultantibus conniveant, eorum dissimulationem nefaria perfidia non carere affirmem ; quia populi libertatem cui se, Dei ordinatione, Tutores positos norunt, fraudulenter produnt.* He is clear, that the Estates in Parliament, not only may, but are *Gods Ordinance* for it, and are bound to resist, and not suffer the destruction of Liberties, by exorbitating Princes.

Sect. 2. Object. *But some say they cannot see how the Monarchies mentioned in Scripture, who were not to be resisted, can be Absolute according to our description of Absoluteness :* Why not ? *In Absolute Monarchy there are no limits but the Monarchs own Will, but these had a fixed Judicial Law.*

Answ. That *Judicial Law* was no limits of their Power, but of the *exercise only*; for the non-observance of it by the King did not amount to an untying of the *Bond of Subjection* in the People, the Judicial Laws being from God, not from any Contract of the People, were in the same nature to that People, and for the time, with the Moral Laws ; and in the same manner did limit their Kings, and no otherwise. But for the *Absoluteness* of that Monarchy, here *Lyra* in 1 *Sam.* 8. *Constitutio Regis juxta potestatem sibi concessam est duplex.* 1. *Plena & legibus absoluta, prout legista de Imperatore dicere solent.* 2. *Cum potestate limitata.* Now sayes he, the people sinned, not simply in asking a King ; but in asking a King of the first sort, *to judge them as the Nations*, that is, Absolutely. He is express, 1. That limitation of power makes a limited Monarch. 2. That *Israel* desiring such a Government as the adjacent Nations, desired an absolute Monarch. And indeed as the definement of the *Moral* Law doth not disparage the Absoluteness of the Monarch, because it is from God, not the peoples ; so did not their *Judicial* for the same Reason.

From the lawfulness of resistance of *unreasonable Acts of Will* in an Absolute Monarchy, where *Reason is the Princes Law* ; I may *a fortiori* conclude the lawfulness of resisting of Instruments of *illegal Acts* in a limited Monarchy, where the *Law* of the *Land* is the *Princes Law and Bounds.*

CHAP. V.

Concerning Resistance forbidden, Rom. 13. *And the Reasons for and against Resistance considered.*

Sect. 1. BUT our Opponents principal strength against Resistance, is *Rom.* 13. from whence nothing can be collected against any Resistance, but that which is of *the Powers of the Ordinance*; but that which I defend is of neither of them. Now supposing the truth which I have made good, that in a limited State the limitation is of the Power it self, and not only of the Exercise; it follows evidently that in such a State Resistance of destructive Instruments, is neither of *Power* nor *Gods Ordinance*.

Neither they then, nor we now; not that *Enslaved Senate*, nor our *Free Parliaments*; no Cause, no Priviledge can justifie *Resistance of the Powers of the Ordinance of God*. Yea, I ascribe more to Gods Ordinance of Power, than Dr. *Ferne*, &c. He says that in a limited State we owe only *Passive Subjection* to exceeding Commands of a Prince, by promise limiting himself in the use of his power; I say, though he sin in exceeding such promise; yet we owe him also *Active Obedience* in such Commands which Gods Law forbids us not to be *active* in. He makes no distinction of *States*, but expounds the Text in question, speaking of Gods Ordinance in general in all Rulers.

In limited Monarchies, where the Prince hath no Authority beyond the Law: There an Act beyond the Law is unauthoritative and meerly private; so that it is no *abusing of Authority*, but an *exceeding of Authority*: Authority abused to undue acting of matters within its compass, Mr. *Burroughs* speaks of, and that must not be resisted. But the Princes Will acting against his Law, that is, matter without the compass of Authority, is not Gods Ordinance, says Dr. *Bilson*, and so may be resisted in its Instruments.

Object. But it is said, (1.) *In that Government under which the Apostles lived, men might not resist, though the Powers commanded contrary to Law, as oft they did: Not under the* Arrian *Emperours, though Religion was then a part of the Law.*

Ans. 1. Dr. *Abbot* Bishop of *Sarum* was of another Judgment; *Demonstrat Antichri. cap.* 7. In that Government he doth distinguish the Christians carriage according to the distinction of times. At first before Religion was established by Law, *cædebantur non cædebant*, but after *Constantines* time when it was established by Law, *cædebant, non cædebantur*. 2. We may grant it in that Government, because it was absolute, and the Laws were to the Prince but *moral* limitations of *exercife* : And acts of the Princes Will, exceeding such limitation, are *Poteſtative*, and must not be reſiſted: But it will not follow that therefore they are ſo, in Governments where the Laws are limitations of the power it ſelf, and *exceeding* acts are not *Poteſtative* : Sure in thoſe times, as patient as the Chriſtians were under their Perſecutors, if their Religion and perſons had been aſſaulted without Authority, they would have made Reſiſtance; and this is all we affirm.

Some alſo there are who quere and ſay;

(1.) How can the putting down of *Epiſcopal Government* be now *juſtified*, which ſtands by Law ?

Anſw. It cannot, unleſs there be a confluence of the conſent of all three; nor do I believe it is intended without the Kings conſent; unleſs their conſtant Doctrine and Practice to overthrow the Liberties and Government of this Kingdom into Arbitrarineſs, do prove them in all their ſort ſubverſive and inconſiſtent with its ſafe being; let them therefore look how they continue to maintain ſuch *deſtructive Doctrines*, for they will ſooner remove themſelves out of this Church, than the Subjects out of their antient and juſt Liberties.

(2.) They ſay, *The Apoſtle in his reaſon againſt Reſiſtance hath no reſpect to the abſolute or limited condition of thoſe Roman Emperours* ; nor do I ſay, he hath ; the reaſon they urge is the *Ordinance of God*, which is true without diſtinction of the whole latitude of power.

(3.) They ſay, *A limited condition doth no more infer a lawfulneſs of reſiſtance for exorbitancies then an abſolute* : I ſay not, that it doth, no condition can infer a lawfulneſs of reſiſtance of the power, though abuſed ; but here is the *priviledge* of a people under a limited *Monarch*, his exceeding acts are not abuſes of power ; but ſimply *non poteſtative* ; and therefore their Agents may be reſiſted, without reſiſting the power ; which is not ſo in an *abſolute Rule* ; if there were no priviledge, why did men trouble themſelves in conſtituting limitations, and mixtures in a State : In a word, unleſs you can prove power in all limited States, to be ill limited ; and all the Acts of Will in the Supream to flow from *Gods Ordinance*, you labour in vain from that Text, or any elſe, to conclude againſt Reſiſtance of ſubverſive Inſtruments in a mixed Government.

Let us here do two things.

(1.) Conſider Reaſons againſt Reſiſtance.

(2.) Conſider Anſwers to thoſe brought for it, but for more evident proceeding about both, we muſt diſtinctly call to mind the Queſtion of what it is. 1. It is of Reſiſtance *in this State* ; that is, a State which I have proved to be *limited* and *mixed* in the very *Power* it ſelf. 2. It is only of *Reſiſtance of deſtructive Inſtruments* ; therefore if the Reaſons do not reach to ſuch a Reſiſtance, they are not to the purpoſe. The Reaſons againſt Reſiſtances are ;

1. *From the Wisdom of God putting his people under Kings, without power of Resistance.*

Answ. 1. It was their defire to be under an abfolute Government, as their neighbour Countreys were; and they offended God in it, as *Lyra* obferves: therefore he giving them fuch a King as they defired, did not in his Wifdom intend a *binding Form* for all people: I think none will affirm he did. (2.) If he mean *Refiftance* of their *Prince, his Authority and Perfon.* I grant they were fo put under; and fo are we, and all that are put under *Monarchs*; but if you mean the Acts of the Princes Will which were not Authoritative; I do deny it, and the inftances in this Treatife alledged prove they were not, and that is all I affirm in other Monarchies.

2. *The Word of God gives no direction for it, the Prophets call not on the Elders for it: the New Teftament commends patience in fuffering for well doing.*

Answ. 1. In Civil matters negative reafonings from Scripture are not proving. (2.) The Word gives proving and imitable examples for it, and indeed the Scripture doth every way juftifie refiftance of Cut-Throats and private deftructive Affaulters of Laws and Liberties, who have no Authority derived to them; and I defend no other.

3. *The Apoftle forbids refiftance of the Powers, not from any compact of the people, but from the Ordinance of God.* It is true, for no compact of people could eftablifh an unrefiftable power without the *Ordinance of God.* I acknowledge the Apoftles ground for it, and therefore allow no refiftance where there is *Gods Ordinance* to fecure them, not for any abufe.

4. *To be Supream and next to God implyes a fecurity from Refiftance.* I grant all; his *Perfon*, his *Powers* is hereby fecured: I condemn all rifing up againft the *King*, but inftruments of fubverfion have nothing of the King in them, not his *Perfon* nor *Authority* is rifen up againft, in them. Neither do I give to the *Houfes*, the power of the *Lacedemonian Ephori.* They had an Authority over the very perfon of the King: which the Houfes claim not. I give them no more then *Calvin* doth to the Three Eftates in their General Meetings. Could any prove that a limited Prince could commit *Power* to do Acts without the bounds of his *Power*, the queftion were anfwered. Some make no difference between Acts exceeding *bounds* of power: and acts of *abufed power.* *He that bears the Sword*, that is, *hath the fupream power, gives Commiffion to under-Minifters for Juftice; and to other Officers for the Militia: if therefore the Refiftance of thofe though abufing their power be a Refiftance of the Power; fo it is alfo of thefe.* *Answ.* I grant all, for it proceeds only of Minifters *abufing power* committed to them, not of exceffes of power. I will retort it, like as if when the *Supream* gives *Commiffion of Juftice* to a *Judge*; and he exceeding unto acts without the Compafs of his Commiffion is but a private man in thofe Acts and may be refifted: fo if *Commiffion of Arms* be given to a *General*, &c.

5. *Sub-*

5. *Subjection is due to a Prince, and the contrary forbidden without diſtinction of a good and bad Prince.* I grant it, and give the reaſon, becauſe they are *Gods Ordinance*, but the queſtion is of inſtruments of exceeding Acts, in which they are not Gods Ordinance.

6. *Good reaſon that he which hath the Supream Truſt, ſhould have the greateſt ſecurity.* *Anſwer.* It is ſo; and ſo we grant him, for he hath full ſecurity from all violence for both *Perſon* and *Authority*, whatever exorbitancy he breaks out unto. The people have not ſo, every ſubject being under the penalty of the Law for its tranſgreſſions. But he is not arguing for ſecurity of *Soveraigns*; but *Subjects*, if they may be ſo call'd, which endeavour to ſubvert Laws and Governments. But may we not alſo ſay, as it is good reaſon the Supream ſhould have the greateſt ſecurity; ſo the people alſo ſhould have ſome ſecurity; and not to be expoſed like brute Beaſts to the ſavage luſts of every inſtrument of cruelty: having only this to comfort them, that they ſin in ſo doing? And ſo they do, which with cruelty deſtroy even the brute Creatures.

7. *From the end and benefits of Government, for the enjoying of which, it is good reaſon we ſhould bear with the exorbitancies.*

Still he ſpeaks *good reaſon*; but nothing to the purpoſe, for we diſpute not of *exorbitancies* of them who have the power; but of them who have no power for what they do. In exorbitancies of leſſer nature, their will may ſecure inſtruments, but it is againſt reaſon that the benefits we have by their Government ſhould cauſe to bear with them who would deſtroy their Laws and Government, for of ſuch is the Queſtion.

8. *Power of Reſiſtance in Subjects would be a remedy worſe than the diſeaſe, and more ſubverſive of a ſtate, than if it were left without it.* Why would it be ſo? *It would be a continual Seminary of jealouſies betwixt Prince and People, and confuſion through the continuance of the miſchiefs of War.* Concerning this Argument ſee *Part. 2. Chap. 5. Sect. 4. Treat.* Where it is fully ſatisfied, (1.) Who will believe the power of reſiſting deſtructive Inſtruments ſhould be more deſtructive, than to let them alone without reſiſtance? (2.) Suppoſe by *abuſe of this power* thoſe evils ſhould happen (for it ſo fails out to the beſt Phyſick, where the Nocumentous humours are prevailing) yet this is but by accident; ſuch power *per ſe* and of its own nature tends to the preventing of ſubverſion. On the contrary by woful experience, this Doctrine of the unreſiſtableneſs of ſuch men, hath nurſed up a brood of Audacious projectors, and where it is taught a *State* will never be without them, whereas if the Truth were known it would reſtrain the ſpirits of wicked men from *Parricide* and *State Subverſion*. Neither can any thing be more miſchievous, than to teach an impunity for projectors, and Agents of miſchief; and he hath not the Reaſon of a man who argues otherwiſe. (3.) Neither can this Doctrine as the Replyer traduceth it, extend to the *depoſing of Princes.*

Princes, or the *diminishing* of their Authority, for it concerns only their *Instruments*, not their *Persons*; their Absolute, extra-legal *Will*, not their *Authority*. And for jealousies, they will be more bred by that Doctrine which gives the *Prince* a Power to undoe the *State*, then by that which terminates both; and gives *neither* a Power to subvert the *other* : Danger is the cause of Jealousie, that which takes away *power of hurting* takes away *danger*; and so removes jealousies; but indeed such which have a plot of breaking up the hedge of Government, and bringing Lawless Powers into a State, care not for having such a Power in those *Houses* whom it would cause them to fear, and look on with *continual jealousies*. The *Homily* of Rebellion is in vain cited against that which is no Rebellion.

We come next (2.) to consider Answers to my Reasons for Resistance, Part 2. Chap. 5.

To the third ; *Such Power is due to a publick State*, &c. is answered, *This is not universally true.* Why not ? A State is more worthy, and comprehends a multitude of particular Men ; doth number detract from their *priviledge* ? He would seem to have reason for his denyal : *A private man hath by the Law of Nature power of self-preservation against the force of another private man*; *yet is this Power yielded up in regard of Civil Power, and not to be used against Persons endued with such Power.*

(1.) Here is still truth ; but not to the question, which is not of persons *indued with Civil Power*, but such as we have proved to have no *Power* ; grant them *endued with Power*, neither a particular man or a whole Community must resist them ; but having none, it is much more allowable in a *publick* State, than in a *particular* Person.

(2.) He speaks of a *Power yielded up,* as if in all Governments the People do simply yield up all power of Resistance into a full subjection unto all acts of the Princes Will ; whereas we have proved, that in limited Governments it is not so ; but to the Princes Will measured and regulated by a Law ; and therefore they have that Power still, in respect of all Instruments of acts of Will not so regulated. Here also because it is said, this *Liberty which I allow a State for its preservation, tends rather to its subversion,* and some every where calumniate us, as inducers of *Confusion* and *Anarchy*, and our Assertions as opening a way to *Rebellion*. It concerns me effectually to vindicate my self, and the truth which I maintain from these aspersions ; and make it appear that the power of Resistance I defend, is not a remedy worse than the disease of subversion ; which I can do no better way then by a positive setting down the naked truth, which I averr ; and shew how it shuts up every way to these evils which they lay uncharitably to our charge.

(1.) I assert no forceable Resistance in any case but *subversive* and *extream.*

(2.) Sub-

(2) Subversive and extream Cases respect either particular men, or the whole State and Government: For *particular men*, even in extream Cases of State or Life, I allow no publick Resistance, but Appeal if it may be had, or if not, yet no publick Resistance; for whether the wrong be done him by Inferiour or Superiour Magistrates; either it is, 1. Under form and course of Law, and Power committed them; and then to resist, is to resist the Power. 2. Or without all form and course of Law, and Power committed to them; and then a Man values his State and Life too high to make publick Resistance, and bring on the State a *general disturbance* for his *private good*, and sins, though not against Gods Ordinance of Power, in this case, yet against the *Publick Peace and Weal*: For the *whole State or Government*, and the last Cases of its subversion, of which our *Antagonists* put the Question:

1. I condemn all force used against the Person of the Supream, or his Power and Authority in any Inferiour Ministers thereof.

2. I averr not publick forceable Resistance of Ministers of Acts of Will, which are only *actual Invasions*, or *excesses of limitation*; and not such as plainly argue a *bent of subversion*, and apparent danger thereof, if prevention be not used.

3. I affirm not force in this utmost case, to be assumed by *private Men*, against destructive Instruments of the Princes Will; as if any Man were warranted on his own imagination of publick danger to raise Forces for prevention. But the *Courts of Justice*, and especially the *Supream Court*, to whom the *Conservation* of *Government* and *Law* is committed, and a power not only to resist, but also censure and punish its Violaters, much more its Subverters, without regard of *Number* or *Warrant*: (The Law supposing no Warrant can be in such case.) This is the Power of Resistance, which I have asserted, and if this be inducing of *Civil War*, or a *way to Subversion and Rebellion*; it is a *War* raised by *Defenders of Law* against *Subverters of Law*; a *Rebellion* raised by *Magistrates having Authority*, against *Instruments of Arbitrariness having no Authority*; a Resistance tending to subversion, but of none but subverters. It is good reason then, it seems, if destroyers grow to the number and strength of an Army; for Magistrates to let them alone, and not raise Arms to suppress them, least they open a way to confusion, and bring on the miseries of a Civil War. This is their *preservative Doctrine*, and my contrary is *destructive*.

4. From the power of *Inferiour Courts* to punish violaters of Law; though pretending a Warrant of the King —— It is said, *This Argument is inconsequent to prove Power of raising Armies to oppose the Forces of their Sovereign*; I say it concludes it *inevitably*; for if the Kings Warrant to violate Law, will not priviledge *one* from force of Justice, then not a hundred, not an Army of Violaters; their *multitude* makes the danger *greater*, and the

Kingdom more unhappy; not Malefactor: *iledged*. The *Forces of the Sovereign* in truth, *are the Forces raise* ! *his Government*; not those which are raised to subvert it. Th ʿ which have his *Authoritative Will*; not those which have only his *Arbitrary*. If ever Reasons did demonstrate a truth, I am confident these four have made good *the Power of the Estates in Parliament to resist subversive Instruments be they more or fewer.* Phil. 4. 5. *Let your moderation be known unto all men: The Lord is at hand.*

F I N I S.

www.ingramcontent.com/pod-product-compliance
Lightning Source LLC
Chambersburg PA
CBHW020858160426
43192CB00007B/975